IN
ESSENTIALS,
UNITY

An Ecumenical Sampler

by Edward A. Powers

FRIENDSHIP PRESS   New York

Unless otherwise stated, all Bible quotations used in this book are from the Revised Standard Version, copyright 1946 and 1952, by the Division of Christian Education of the National Council of the Churches of Christ in the United States of America.

Library of Congress Cataloging in Publication Data

In essentials, unity.

  Includes bibliographical references.
    1. Christian union—Addresses, essays, lectures.
  2. Church and social problems—Addresses, essays, lectures.
  3. Litanies. I. Powers, Edward A.
  BX9.I48   280'.042   82-1446
  ISBN: 0-377-00117-1   AACR2

Editorial Office: 475 Riverside Drive, Room 772, New York, NY 10115
Distribution Office: PO Box 37844, Cincinnati, OH 45237

Printed in the United States of America.

CONTENTS

To the Reader:

This book may be used as a map of the ecumenical territory conveying many of the current contours and routes which people are taking in their communities, regions, and around the globe. It can be used to sample the agenda of Christians seeking unity and common mission. Think of it as a mirror in the manner of the following illustration from the New York Times:

Back when Poland was a different country—which is to say, eight months before the strikes of last year set off a chain of events that is shaking Poland's foundations and posing the most serious threat to the Soviet Union in decades — an exhibition called "The Polish People — Self-Portrait" ran at the National Gallery in Cracow. It drew huge crowds. People came from all over to see it, and they waited in line, a thousand at a time.

What they saw when they got inside were hundreds of paintings and photographs of Poles down through the ages: kings, noblemen, workers, peasants, revolutionaries, soldiers, priests. The next-to-last portrait was an impressionistic painting, clearly of Pope John Paul II, entitled "Pole of the Year." The last picture at the exhibition didn't bear any title at all—it was simply a mirror.

Though they may have bypassed one or two portraits on display, everyone stopped in front of the mirror. As they peered into it, what reflections did they see? Themselves in the ermine of kings, or wrapped in cloaks concealing revolvers as they planned to assassinate the czar, or in a bishop's mantle and miter — or, as they were, in peasant garb, workers' coveralls, or business suits? Whatever the reflection, the message was unmistakable. "You are part of a great and varied lineage with one thing in common — you are all Poles."[1]

We take the ecumenical journey as pilgrims and colleagues of the one who prayed "that they may all be one..." The quest and gift of unity mirror us.

Do everything in common;
Unite in one prayer, one petition,
one mind, one hope,
in love and faultless joy.
All this is Jesus Christ
and there is nothing better than he.
So make haste, all of you,
to come together as to one temple of God,
around one altar,
around the one Jesus Christ...

St. Ignatius of Antioch (115 A.D.)
Letter to the Manesians

1.
Christian Unity Is a Fact

In the heart of the seventeenth century struggle for religious freedom in Great Britain during the Reformation, the Puritan Richard Baxter wrote:

> In essentials, unity;
> In non-essentials, liberty;
> In all things, charity.

His first phrase titles this book, a catalog of issues on the ecumenical agenda. The book is meant to be savored, tasted, and sampled as readers catch the spirit of churches and church folk as together they address life issues.

Often the Baxter quote has been used to define matters of faith. The essentials underlined in this book are about faith and its application in a wide range of human issues. Catch the heartbeat of the ecumenical movement—food offered by churches together to hungry people, tangible assistance to homeless people in Southeast Asia, Africa and the Middle East, community celebrations of the arts, actions for social justice, dialogue fostered by Christians among people with ancient enmities toward each other, and the search for a common biblical text through which the Spirit speaks in our time. It is in just such actions as these that the One Church of Jesus Christ will manifest its God-given unity in the world, if it is to be manifested at all.

This is a practical book. It is faithful to the agreements which Christians have forged in their various ecumenical councils through the centuries. But its focus is upon the issues which Christians are facing together and the ways they are acting in concert to make the world a better place. Its theme is that Christian unity is a fact now wherever Christians seek together to make a difference.

The Common Ground
World Council of Churches/Roman Catholic Church

Despite all divisions which have occurred in the course of the centuries, there is a real though imperfect communion which continues to exist among those who believe in Christ and are baptized in his name. They confess that Christ, true God and true Man, is Lord and that it is through him and in him alone that we are saved. Through the Spirit, they offer praise and thanksgiving to the Father who, in his Son, reconciles the world to himself. They proclaim the love of God, revealed by the Son who was sent by the Father, bringing new life to the human race, and who through the promise and gift of the Holy Spirit gathers together the people of the New Covenant as a communion of unity in faith, hope, and love.

Through the development of the ecumenical movement that communion has been experienced anew. This is not to claim that it has been created anew. Since it is beyond human power and initiative, it precedes all ecumenical effort for the restoration of the unity of all Christians. The gift of communion God has bestowed in Jesus Christ remains a reality even where Christians may obscure or damage it by their lack of understanding, their disobedience and mutual estrangement. The ecumenical movement is therefore the common rediscovery of that existing reality and equally the common effort to overcome the obstacles standing in the way of perfect communion. It is at the same time a return and a new departure.

The joy of the ecumenical movement lies in the fact that the power of this communion has become more evident among the churches. Christians have been gathered together. They have been enriched in their experience and have been given new strength.

The nature of the communion by which we are held together cannot yet be described together in concrete terms. The language we use is marked by the divisions of history. Each church has its own approach and its own terminology. But since the churches meet in Christ's name and share in his gift, their fellowship must have reality. As they move forward together, both the nature of the present communion they already have and the future unity they seek may become clearer and their divisions may be healed.[2]

The Essence of the Ecumenical Movement

The ecumenical movement is central to the life of the church. It bears witness in the midst of our several Christian communities and traditions to a miracle of divine grace: that Jesus calls us, by his death, resurrection, and continuing life among us out of our alienation and ignorance of each other into loving and creative relationships.

It reminds us that the gift of baptism makes us one with Christ our brother and it makes us sisters and brothers of each other: that our traditions, stripped of unholy superficialities, cannot remain barriers but have riches to be shared. It calls each Christian community to be true in life and action to her own profession of commitment to Christ's mission of reconciliation, peace, and justice for all people.[3]

Donald Anderson, Canadian Council of Churches

Karl Barth on Separation and Unity

There is no justification, theological, spiritual, or biblical for the existence of a plurality of Churches genuinely separated in this way and mutually excluding one another internally and therefore externally. A *plurality* of Churches in this sense means a plurality of *lords*, a plurality of *gods*. There is no doubt that to the extent that Christendom does consist of actually different and opposing *Churches*, to that extent it denies practically what it confesses theoretically—the unity and the singularity of God, of Jesus Christ, of the Holy Spirit. There may be good grounds for the rise of these divisions. There may be serious obstacles to their removal. There may be many things which can be said by way of interpretation and mitigation. But this does not alter the fact that every division as such is a deep riddle, a *scandal*.[4]

Two Cups, Three Cities

This poignant story of brokenness and unity unites Christians across the oceans and leaps the Berlin Wall.

One of the high moments of the United Church of Christ's Synod in the early summer of 1981 came following a vote to acknowledge the special bond between the Evangelische Kirche der Union of Germany and the United Church of Christ. The relationship of the two churches both historic and contemporary was expressed through President

Joachim Rogge of East Berlin (EKU) and President Avery D. Post (UCC).

After the vote, four ecumenical visitors were ushered onto the stage by members of the joint working group as delegates broke into the doxology. There were greetings.... There was an exchange of gifts. As Avery Post gave each of the four guests a UCC pendant cross, the delegates applauded, German style, and then broke spontaneously into "They'll Know We Are Christians by Our Love." The Germans presented the UCC with a chalice and paten...to be used in communion services at future Synods. Then the UCC returned the gesture. Another cup and plate — symbolic of *Kirchengemeinschaft*, full communion. There had been no advance discussion of the gifts. In both churches the communion sets seemed appropriate tokens of the theological and spiritual unity that has developed for more than a quarter of a century.

There was a special poignancy in the set that the Germans will carry home. The EKU is a single church, but it has been forced since the building of the Berlin Wall to meet in two synods. The cup will go to East Berlin, the paten to West Berlin. The communion set is thus also a symbol of hope. of longing for the time when the synods of the EKU will be reunited.[5]

Humanity's Divisions and Christian's Unity

God's great gift in Jesus Christ is the promise of a new community in which humanity's estrangements are overcome. The churches are called to seek to give visible institutional form to this new community in a manner which will enable their members in each place to gather around the Word and sacraments and to work out their mission in the world together.

God calls the Church into the world to build personal and corporate community, in creating structures of justice and service, in mediating reconciliation. But each of these commissions of Christ is called into question and crippled in implementation by our divisions. By their disunity and competition the churches make fully authentic witness or community impossible and their resources are squandered in an irresponsible fashion.[6]

World Council of Churches,
Fifth Assembly, Nairobi,
Kenya, 1975

Churchly Solidarity in Poland

When we enter the Church we are in the zone of light, we are in a sanctuary where we dare to be ourselves, where we feel accepted. This is the only place where there is no waiting line to get what we need, where we are not told to come next day because the service is over for today (as we are likely to be told in all secular "service stations"...). Jesus is always there and accessible to all. Jesus, the Advocate, Healer, Friend, and Saviour, Son of Mary who intercedes for those who pray.

And if it is so, if the Church is there as a holy sign of the kingdom, then the Church can also in some way lift people's hearts, sustain them so that they become more able to get out of frustration in a spirit of sacrifice. This spirit for us means to be involved in some kind of resistance against corruption, against universal frustration and negligence, against giving up. It encourages people to engage in action for survival as a community, for defense of dignity and identity—to be subjects and not mere objects of historical processes. Instead of suffering it all for nothing, we take responsibility for the direction of the life of our community. This is painful and costly and risky but immensely different from submission which breaks the spirit and deprives life of meaning.[7]

The Church in Poland, 1981

Litany—What Unity Requires

Leader: Let us thank God that we are made in the divine image and belong to one another. Let us thank God for new creation, making us one in Christ.

People: There can be no thanks without giving, no words without deeds that are done.

Leader: Let us thank God that Christians of different traditions are learning to understand one another better. Let us pray for our local congregations that they may grow closer together.

People: There can be no thanks without giving, no words without deeds that are done.

Leader: Let us thank God for our churches, and pray that we and all their members may be so filled with the spirit of faith, hope, and love, that people may recognize the reality of the Gospel.

People: There can be no thanks without giving, no words without deeds that are done.

Leader: Let us pray for our local communities, thanking God for all that is done to help people to live harmoniously together.

People: There can be no thanks without giving, no words without deeds that are done.

Leader: Let us pray for our nation and thank God for all who work to bring about greater understanding between the young and the old, between employers and employed, between immigrants and host communities, and between the Church and those who have rejected institutional Christianity.

People: There can be no thanks without giving, no words without deeds that are done.

Leader: Let us thank God for our world, and pray for its unity, for reconciliation and peace, for justice and compassion, between rich and poor, black and white, left and right.

People: There can be no thanks without giving, no words without deeds that are done.

Unison: Lord, in your mercy, hear our prayer and enable us to translate our thanksgiving into selfless discipleship.

Amen[8]

2.
Ecumenism—What's In A Word?

The subtitle of this book is "An Ecumenical Sampler." What's in the word ECUMENICAL? Well, it's an old Greek word that means "the whole inhabited earth." It has been used since the Fourth Century to describe the unity, the wholeness of the church. For example, the Council of Nicea which produced the Nicene Creed in 325 A.D. is called the first ecumenical council.

Sometimes today the word is defined as any activities which Christians and churches from different traditions do together. More often it refers to the actions of religious organizations which gather many churches together such as the Texas Conference of Churches or the Canadian Council of Churches or the World Council of Churches. In its largest sense it refers to the pressure toward and experience of the unity of Christian people which is both Christ's gift and calling.

The word ecumenical is also used in geography and ecology. There it means the forces — human and natural — that sustain life. Thus, the fullest use of the term is the unity and concern for the ecosystem, the inhabited earth. Economics is a close linguistic cousin of ecumenical. Their relationship reminds us that how we live together and what the structures are that bind us together are faith's concerns.

The Ecumenical Movement is the name given to the Christian forces for unity which are expressed both structurally in united church structures and in common action. In a larger sense it is the cluster of forces which drive and bind the churches to work together in service of a common Lord. That movement understands "the whole inhabited earth" as its concern.

We often speak of the modern ecumenical movement, a twentieth century phenomenon, which has roots in both a faith and order tradition, and a life and work tradition. The former has worked on ways to overcome separation in areas of doctrine, structure, ministry, sacraments, and churchly practice. The latter has given attention to the ways in which Christians can join together in common witness and action in their communities and around the world.

This sampler displays the meaning of ecumenical by relating it to a number of issues which affect people. We will explore the issue, see what ecumenical church bodies have said about it, and review some samples. Our hope is to give flesh and blood reality to an important word.

An Australian Creed of Hope

I believe in God
  and I believe in humanity
  as the image of God.

In believe in Australians
  in their black aboriginal
    beauty
  in their migrant struggles
  as they come into their own
  having given up their own.

I believe in Australian life
  as a search for identity
  not a short-term loan
    threatened by drought,
      invasion or cynicism
  but a gift with its purposes

I believe in the Australian
  place
  with its Asian context and its
    northern culture
  with all its nearness and its
    distance
  with all its possibilities for
    growth and decline
  in dream time, southern
    time, our time.

I believe in our responsibility
  for creation
  the trust of every mountain
    range

of every forest
of every harbour
of every city
of every plan
to build a future
as Adams of today.

I believe in our hopes for a
  great human family
  as Christ wishes it
  in hopes fostered by
    memories
  and banishing from the land
    of the Holy Spirit
  the stupor of despair.

I believe in myself
  in the mobility that God has
    bestowed on me
  the experience of the greatest
    of all joys
  to give myself
  on my road to Emmaus and
    Jericho

And I hope for living waters
  to flow from the dead heart
    of Christ
  and transform our heart of
    death
  into the image of the risen
    God.[1]

LITANY OF WALLS AND UNITY

Leader: Lord, you made the world and everything in it; you created the human race of one stock and gave us the earth for our possession.

People: Break down the walls that separate us and unite us in a single body.

Leader: Lord, we have been divisive in our thinking, in our speech, in our actions; we have classified and imprisoned one another; we have fenced each other out by hatred and prejudice.

People: Break down the walls that separate us and unite us in a single body.

Leader: Lord, you mean us to be a single people, ruled by peace, feasting in freedom, freed from injustice, truly human, men and women, responsible and responsive in the life we lead, the love we share, the relationships we create.

People: Break down the walls that separate us and unite us in a single body.

Leader: Lord, we shall need ever-new insights into the truth, awareness of your will for all humanity, courage to do what is right even when it is not allowed, persistence in undermining unjust structures until they crumble into dust, grace to exercise a ministry of reconciliation.

People: Break down the walls that separate us and unite us in a single body.

Leader: Lord, share out among us the tongues of your Spirit, that we may each burn with compassion for all who hunger for freedom and humanness; that we may be doers of the Word and so speak with credibility about the wonderful things you have done.

All: Lord, direct us in ways we do not yet discern and equip us for the service of reconciliation and liberation in your world.[2]

3.
The Mandate

The movement for Christian unity is not just a game played by people who like that sort of thing. The mandate comes from the gospel itself. Jesus' prayer the last night of his earthly life included these urgent words:

I do not pray for these only [the disciples]. . . but also for those who believe in me through their word, that they may all be one; even as thou, Father, art in me, and I in thee, that they may also be in us, so that the world may believe that thou has sent me.

The unity is "that the world may believe." It is not unity for its own sake. The credibility of church and faith are at stake. In the early centuries of the church's life, the pagan world noted, "See how these Christians love one another!"

Paul uses the metaphor of the body in Romans 12:

For as in one body we have many members, and all the members do not have the same function, so we, though many, are one body in Christ, and individually members one of another.

The Letter to the Ephesians conveys similar conviction:

I therefore, a prisoner for the Lord, beg you to lead a life worthy of the calling to which you have been called, with all lowliness and meekness, with patience, forbearing one another in love, eager to maintain the unity of the Spirit in the bond of peace. There is one body and one Spirit, just as you were called to the one hope that belongs to your call, one Lord, one faith, one baptism, one God and Father of us all, who is above all and through all and in all.

Traditions

An underlying premise is that there is one Lord, one Faith, one Baptism, one Church but many churches and forms of ministry. We often speak of Tradition with a capital "T" meaning the common core of Christian experience, faith, and community through the centuries. In *contrast*, there are traditions (small "t"), which reflect the ways individual denominations express the one faith.

Much of our energy and imagination is given to enlarging our common roots and understanding the unity that is God-given.

This search for common unity is not an attempt to clone Christians in a single form. It honors the faithful diversity through which Christians seek to express the faith in each place in their own time.

Unity is not uniformity of form, interpretation, or style. It is the recovery through the grace of God of our common humanity and uniting faith.

Our vision of the future is that we shall once again live as brothers and sisters in one undivided Church. The one Church is to be envisioned as a conciliar fellowship of local churches which are themselves truly united. In this conciliar fellowship each local church possesses, in communion with the others, the fulness of catholicity, witnesses to the same apostolic faith and therefore recognizes the others as belonging to the same Church of Christ and guided by the same Spirit...[1]

Faithfulness in Ministry

Faithfulness requires the churches to recognize that the unity of the church is essential to their ministry. Faithfulness to Christ requires them to claim a renewed understanding of the biblical mandate for Christian unity, and to allow this mandate to mature in their faith and work; to confront in penitence their preoccupation with denominational self-interests and to grow toward a full sharing in faith and mission, reflective to the full unity which Christ has given. The churches can no longer accept as inevitable their historical divisions over matters of faith, worship and mission. Their calling to live out this unity is the task of the whole people of God and not merely the responsibility of its professional leaders.

Faithfulness requires the National Council to be an unashamed advocate of Christian unity and to claim this gift as an essential part of any national ecumenical body. It cannot allow the churches to use the council as a stage from which they "are not quite divided while remaining far from united..." The National

19

Council is a community where the churches seek to grow toward the one church, and where together the witness of the churches is made to the nation.[2]

The Christian faith is a uniting faith. It draws people together because Jesus Christ is like a magnet. As we draw closer to him, we are inevitably drawn closer together.

But, the God who through grace draws us closer also sends us forth. The Christian faith is a reaching out, sharing, serving, sending faith. Jesus came (John 3:16) that the world might be saved. Thus, it is to the unbelieving world that the Christian is sent.

The Task of Reconciliation

The objective of the ecumenical movement will always remain the same: to reconcile and reunite groups of Christians who have been apart for a long time. The main purpose is to render all baptized people of all denominations, beginning with our own, conscious of the scandal of divisions.

The ecumenical task will need more and more individuals and groups who are deeply motivated and not easily discouraged by difficulties. Christians of all traditions, we have to help one another to strengthen the spir-

itual renewal, the doctrinal research, the dialogue and cooperation at various levels on local, regional, and national scenes.[3]

Your Kingdom Come

The Melbourne conference on evangelism sponsored by the World Council of Churches in May of 1980 focused on one petition of the Lord's Prayer—Your Kingdom Come. The delegates said:

This title is a frightening claim, but a wonderful reality. It is frightening because it causes every one of us to examine our personal experience of the empirical church, and to confess how often our church life has hidden rather than revealed the sovereignty of God. . . . Yet there is reality here. The whole church of God, in every place and time, is a sacrament of the kingdom which came in the person of Jesus Christ and will come in its fulness when he returns in glory.

The life and witness of our present churches is very diverse, and it is not our calling to be judges of their value to God. We can only look at some aspects of that life and witness to see how the church can more effectively carry the marks of Christ himself and be a sign of the kingdom.

The proclamation of the word

of God is one such witness, distinct and indispensable. The story of God in Christ is the heart of all evangelism, and this story has to be told, for the life of the present church never fully reveals the love and holiness and power of God in Christ. The telling of the story is an inescapable mandate for the whole church; word accompanies deed as the kingdom throws its light ahead of its arrival and men and women seek to live in that light.

The church is called to be a community, a living, sharing fellowship. This sign of the kingdom is evident where our churches are truly open to the poor, the despised, the handicapped, for whom our modern societies have little care. Then a church becomes a witness to the Lord who rejoiced in the company of outcasts.[4]

Jesus' Own Gift

We are united in the continuing celebration of the Lord's Supper even when our traditions are separate. The events of Easter and of Jesus' resurrection bind us together as those who have received grace.

Easter begins with celebration, for Easter is the feast where the resurrected Christ makes a thank-offering in gratitude for his resurrection and breaks bread with his disciples. At first, in early Christianity, the epiphanies of Easter and the celebration of the Lord's Supper were joined together. The resurrected Christ, as the leader of life against death, initiates his own into the new life and imparts himself to them in the Lord's Supper.

Therefore the Eucharist is filled with remembrances of the cross and with hope for the new creation. In the unity of remembrance and hope Easter is a demonstration of present rejoicing in grace. It means resurrection, freedom, and joy. But Easter is the resurrection of the crucified Christ. It does not overcome the story of Christ's passion so that we need no longer remember it. Rather, it establishes Christ's cross as a saving event. The one who goes *before us* into the glorious and liberated future of God's resurrected is also the one who died for us on the cross. We come face to face with the glory of the coming God beholding the features of the crucified and not through infinite demands or flights of fancy. His degradation leads to our exaltation. His descent into hell opens the heaven in liberty for those in bondage. So the cross of Christ remains the symbol of hope on earth for those who have been liberated.[5]

Edinburgh to Melbourne

The Journey of the Churches Together in Mission

This has been a long pilgrimage, from Edinburgh to Melbourne—and well should it be, because momentous events have taken place both in the world of peoples and nations and in the churches through the missionary movement. What is remarkable about this period is the extraordinary boldness, courage, courtesy, faith, hope and love displayed by all those who were involved in this great movement. It was William Carey who had said: "Expect great things from God. Attempt great things for God." He was planning a world gathering on mission for 1810 but his dream was not fulfilled until 1910. It was J. H. Oldham who used to say: "We must dare in order to know." In these 70 years many things have been dared in obedience to the Gospel of the Kingdom of God. We can do no less today.[6]

Philip Potter

Litany of Thanksgiving

Leader: (Edinburgh, 1910) O Lord, we give you thanks for those who opened the modern ecumenical era by coming together at Edinburgh. We are grateful for the passion they had to communicate the gospel to every creature.

People: Keep us together, Lord, and rekindle among us such a vision for our day.

Leader: (Jerusalem, 1928) O Lord, we give you thanks for those who went back to Jerusalem and to the sources of our faith, committing themselves to renewal in mission. We are grateful for their courage in facing the realities of a growing technological and industrial world and in defining mission in ways relevant to that new reality.

People: Lord, grant us the same roots in your Word and the same courage to open ourselves to the realities of our time.

Leader: (Tambaram, India, 1938) O Lord, we give you thanks for those who in Tambaram discovered the church as the active bearer of the gospel. We are grateful for their honest attempt to give witness to the uniqueness of Jesus Christ in a world of universal religions.

People: Lord, help us and our churches to discern signs of your kingdom among all cultures and peoples. Help us to give humble witness to our own experience in Christ.

Leader: (Whitby, Canada, 1947) Lord, we give thanks for the recognition at Whitby of churches as partners in obedience to a common missionary calling. We thank you for their readiness to participate in the reconstruction of a world ravaged by war.

People: Lord, help us to realize more fully the meaning of our own partnership, and the peculiar tasks that are ours in the permanent reconstruction of a world ravaged by hate and destruction.

Leader: (Willingen, Federal Republic of Germany, 1952) We worship you, O God, as the missionary God who through your creating, judging, and redeeming action are bringing all things to a final uniting in Christ; and we thank you for the fellowship we enjoy with you and with one another through participation in your mission.

People: Help us, Lord, through the vision of your kingdom to be present with you in your work.

Leader: (Achimota, Ghana, 1957-58) We thank you, O Lord, for the integration of the International Missionary Council into the World Council of Churches. We thank you for the vision of a church united in mission.

People: Grant, O Lord, that the work we do here may enhance the fulfillment of that vision.

Leader: (Mexico City, 1963) We thank you, Lord, for the coming together of Orthodox, Roman Catholic, and Protestant Christians in a common search for missionary obedience. We thank you for the awareness of missionary challenges in every continent.

People: Help us to bring forth the fruits of that diversity in unity for the evangelization of all continents.

Leader: (Bangkok, 1972-73) We thank you, O Lord, for the reality of your salvation manifest in every culture. We thank you for your good news of salvation that sends us in your name into the social, political and cultural struggles of the world.

People: Grant us faithfulness to respond to the grace of your salvation.[7]

4.
We Have This Ministry

The central ministry is that of the whole people of God. Each Christian is called to be a minister (the word means "servant") and every congregation is called to ministry. Ministry is the form of our obedience to the holy God, the pattern of caring for another and for society. It is centered in Christ's own ministry and acts of loving reconciliation.

The ecumenical movement reflects two powerful themes—the ministry of the whole people of God and the steps toward recovering a common ministry of the ordained.

The Canadian Council of Churches and the National Council of Churches held a consultation in 1981 in Toronto to reflect on the nature of the professional ministry today. Here is a summary of delegate conclusions:

The development of a global awareness and a sense of global solidarity among both laity and clergy is an urgent priority and fundamental for everything else we need to do.

We need to give ourselves to the task of visioning, seeking a new understanding of our identity, calling, and ministry. This involves finding new images for the church and ministry through serious biblical and theological study...

Ministry belongs to the LAOS, the whole people of God. Not only must laity be equipped for and supported in ministry, clergy need to develop new styles for being for and with laity who increasingly are feeling the pain of the future.

Economic justice is the central ethical issue in relation to shrinking resources. Ministry must involve serious work on the ethical requirements of global solidarity. Theology needs to be more in dialogue with political economics than it has been in the past.

We must not be diverted from such agendas as racism, sexism, human rights, nationalism, and terrorism. More than ever our image of the church and our dream for society must be both racially and ethnically inclusive and feminized, and our struggle with the issues needs more than ever to be ecumenically open.

We must experiment with and learn new ways to "travel light," to do more with less. This applies not only to personal life style but also to the institutions the church has created.... Our ability to vision and our will to meet the future responsibly are perhaps most severely tested at this point.[1]

The conference impact was summarized in a moving joint statement from two participating denominations. They said:

We dimly perceive that the world may be at the threshold of an era when changes will be of such dimensions and of such consequence to the whole human race that it can best be characterized as a potential wilderness experience; that the pain and anguish of an increasing proportion of humanity constitutes for the church of Jesus Christ an unparalleled opportunity and imperative for ministry in profound new ways; that such ministry is and must become the work of all God's people together; and that the structures of the Church must be kept open for the movement of the Holy Spirit from unexpected quarters.

Therefore, as pilgrim people and in continual responsiveness to the presence of the Spirit we will, with others, seek to discover what this vision may have to say to all that we are called to be and to do.[2]

A Kaleidescope Reflection on Our Common Ministry
Ten Denominations Offer New Hope and Insight

The Consultation on Church Union involves ten denominations in the United States in exploring what a united church will look like. Much of their attention has been given to understanding the nature and shape of Christian ministry. Here is part of their current statement which has two decades of common history behind it:

The life, death and resurrection of Jesus Christ was a ministry of God to all humankind. Through the Holy Spirit, God's people are called to share that ministry and are empowered to fulfill what it requires. By the power of the same Spirit, the ministry of God's People appropriates and continues what God sent Jesus to be and do.

The ministry of Jesus Christ summed up and brought to focus all that God has done in the history of Israel and of all people to set men and women free and to open them both to one another and to God. His was therefore a liberating and reconciling ministry. Sent by God to be and proclaim the fulfillment of all things in God's kingdom, he spoke with the authority of the Servant of God and of humanity.

Accordingly, his mission was to "preach good news to the poor," to "proclaim release to the captives and the recovering of sight to the blind, to set at liberty those who are oppressed, to proclaim the acceptable year of the Lord" (Luke 4:18f; Isaiah 61:1). In him God began to put down "the mighty from their seats," and exalt "those of low degree," to scatter "the proud in the imagination of their hearts," to fill "the hungry with good things and to send the rich empty away." (Luke 1:51–53)

His authority was displayed in his healing the sick, forgiving sins, comforting the afflicted, challenging the arrogant, transforming traditions, and bringing into being a new covenant people in the midst of the old. His authority was also made manifest in his announcement of the end of oppression and of the overturning of unjust power structures through the assertion of God's rule. Through his solidarity with the outcast, and through his compassion for those who oppressed and executed him, he called all humankind to conversion and to repentance and summoned all to glorify God and love one another. In his risen life, Christ's ministry continues both through the life of the Church and through the intercessory role he now exercises in the presence of God.

Answering his gracious summons, Christians by the Spirit are gathered into a ministering community, held together and empowered for service in love, hope, and faith. In Christ, this People's life is vulnerable to suffering, yet strong in the midst of wickedness. It offers and requires relationships of mutuality in need and service, and overcomes despair in the power of hope. This ministry is not confined to those of any one social or ethnic group. It is for and with the whole of humanity. Whenever obedience to Jesus calls his People to be in the world as he was in the world, they are led further by the Spirit into the truth of the Gospel.

Enabled by grace, the People of God enters upon ministry by taking its stand where Christ is at work in the midst of humanity, in a continuing struggle with the powers of this age. This struggle leads to both suffering and joy. Christ's People "complete what remains of Christ's afflictions for the sake of his body, that is, the church" (Col. 1:24). They also know a foretaste of the "joy that was set before him who endured the cross and is set down at the right hand of the throne of God" (Heb. 12:2). Therefore, where women and men struggle against poverty and oppression, ministry means entering into that struggle with oppressor and oppressed alike to overcome the causes of suffering. When men and women engage wittingly or unwittingly in oppressive actions and decisions, ministry means acting compassionately toward them for the eradication of these evils. Where people undergo affliction, pain, disease, and death, ministry means sharing witness with them in the calling to "bear one another's burdens" (Gal. 6:2). Where persons suffer because of their choice to work for liberation and justice, ministry means supporting them in their witness (Phil. 1:29,30; Matt. 25:31–45).

Yet, ministry is not simply to those who suffer and struggle. Those who struggle and suffer without despair may themselves so minister to the world that they offer compelling testimony to the power of the cross and resurrec-

tion. Their ministries may express to the Church the privilege of "dying daily" with Christ, and at the same time of rising with Him to new life. For the ministry of God's people is at the same time joyful. Those who minister in the midst of suffering are called "blessed" (Matt. 5:1–11). They begin to inherit now a kingdom prepared for them before the foundations of the earth (Matt. 25:34). They are offered a foretaste of that messianic banquet at which the poor, the maimed, the blind, and the lame have the privileged place (Luke 14:13–14).

In all its forms and functions, ministry is a rich interweaving of word and worship, work and witness. In different ways, members of the Body share responsibility for the church's government, administration, discipline, instruction, worship, and pastoral care. These activities are held together in a visible ordering through which the Church is equipped for its ministry. "Having gifts that differ according to the grace given to us" (Romans 12:26), the several members bring to the one body a wide diversity of gifts, functions, and services.[3]

Confessing Christ Today
A Litany

Leader: Who are we, Lord, that we should confess to you?
We can hardly speak for ourselves; how could we speak in your name?
We believe in your word but our minds are often full of doubt.
We trust your promises but our hearts are often fearful.
Captivate our minds, Lord, and let your Spirit dwell in our hearts that we may feel and taste your love.

People: For necessity is laid upon us; woe to us if we do not preach the Gospel.

Leader: How can we call new disciples for you, Lord, while our community, your church, is divided and all too conformed to the pattern of this world?
We preach your power of love while we succumb, like all others, to the love of power.
We proclaim your justice while we remain caught up in structures of injustice.
Awaken in us the spirit of unity that we may feel the pain of your body divided, and yearn and reach out for fuller union with you and among ourselves.
Inflame us with the power of your love, that it may consume the vanity of power.
Make us hunger and thirst for justice, that our words may be given authority as signs of your justice.

People: For necessity is laid upon us; woe to us if we do not preach the Gospel.

Leader: How can we sing your song, O Lord, in a strange land?
How can we witness to your all-embracing love with lives full of painful contradictions?
How can we be ambassadors of reconciliation in a world enslaved by sin and death, where children suffer and starve, and many labour in vain while a few live in luxury; where in the midst of our lives we dwell under the shadow of death?
What answer shall we give to the suffering (what shall we say to our own hearts) when they cry from the depths, "Where is now your God?"

People: For necessity is laid upon us; woe to us if we do not preach the Gospel.

Leader: God, mysterious and hidden, you keep us captive while you are the open door, you make us suffer while your suffering heals us, you lead us into the depths of despair while the morning star of hope is shining above us, Lord, crucified, Lord risen: come, transform the necessities that are laid upon us into freedom, joy and praise everlasting. Lord, we believe, help our unbelief.

People: For necessity is laid upon us; woe to us if we do not preach the Gospel.[4]

This litany is one of many in Let's Worship, *in the* Risk *series, an ecumenical worship book first introduced to the Fifth Assembly of the World Council of Churches at Nairobi, Kenya in 1975. Its insights continue to nurture the common life of Christians.*

5.
The Congregation

Christian people gather for worship and fellowship and then scatter to their appointed places of ministry and service. While they are together and when they are scattered their identity remains the same — by their Baptism they are members of the Body of Christ; their membership in a specific congregation marks them a people claimed by God for unique witness.

The New Delhi Assembly of the World Council of Churches in 1961 gave special attention to this witness in a sentence noted both for its length and for the power of its vision:

We believe that the unity which is both God's will and...gift to...[the] Church is being made visible as all in each place who are baptized into Jesus Christ and confess him as Lord and Saviour are brought by the Holy Spirit into one fully committed fellowship, holding the one apostolic faith, preaching the one Gospel, breaking the one bread, joining in common prayer, and having a corporate life reaching out in witness and service to all who at the same time are united with the whole Christian fellowship in all places and all ages in such wise that ministry and members are accepted by all, and that all can act and speak together as occasion requires for the tasks to which God calls...people. [1]

All in each place—one—what a remarkable vision that is! We know all too well how much the full realization of that is in the future tense. Yet, through the Spirit, our awareness of our common humanity in Christ enables us to sense the power and reality of that statement now. Much in

30

our worship life is shared. We participate in common acts of ministry or social justice. Together we welcome a refugee family, oppose an act of prejudice, seek the rights denied to someone, petition for a fair trial for another, or help build a community institution. All in each place are becoming one!

Jesus Christ: Fulfillment of the Covenant

The divine promise of "I will be your God and you shall be my people" has been fulfilled historically in the person of Jesus Christ and in his communion with the Church for the salvation of the world. He came not to destroy the covenant, the law and prophets, but to fulfill them. . . . The new covenant to be ratified by Jesus' blood was promised at the Last Supper with his disciples, made real on the Cross, and vindicated by his being raised from death. Jesus is thus the Mediator of God's gracious covenant, offered to all people: the one giving himself that all might live.

The new covenant took form in a community of faith, starting with the apostles and continuing now and ever. He called them, and calls the church today, to share his mission of suffering and be witness to the Gospel. The Holy Spirit gives people the power to respond in faith. They are brought into the universal community of the new covenant by Baptism in the Spirit, and sustained in communal bond with Christ and one another by the Eucharist.

Biblical teaching places unusual demands upon the church to "maintain the unity of the Spirit in the bond of peace.' Individual members of the body of Christ may have many differences, but in the New Covenant they are one—the new creation—knowing the foretaste of things to come for all creation. This means that the unity of the Church is more binding than cooperation allows, more vital than efficiency suggests. Christ holds us together still in "an everlasting covenant" with sacred bonds to Him, to one another and to all creation. Unity in Christ leaves no room for any autonomy of tradition, culture, ethnicity, race, class, sex, politics (or anything else that we call "Christian pluralism") by which we justify our divisions.

Unity is inherent in the very nature of Christ and the new covenant. It is his gift to us, not our optional achievement. The New

31

Testament conceives that unity not so much as a human association but as having its essential reality in Christ himself in his indissoluble unity with his people. Christ is not divided. As the risen Lord, active by power of the Spirit, he represents and gathers to himself the many women, men and children of redeemed humanity. He alone makes the many to be one in the church.[2]

O Lord, whose holy saints and martyrs in all times and places have endured affliction, suffering, and tribulation, by the power of the Holy Cross, the armour of salvation, so likewise, we pray, send your Holy Spirit, the Comforter and Advocate of all Christians, to sustain these churches in their martyrdom, witness and mission. The world without provocation hates your Church, but you have taught us not to despair. Therefore, you who are a God at hand and not a God afar off, grant to these Christians the power to lift up their hands, their eyes and their hearts to continue their living witness in unity with the universal Church, to the glory of your most holy name.[3]

Prayer of a Contemporary Christian from Romania

6.
The Search for a Living Bible

Oral traditions through which fathers and mothers shared the stories of their faith and God's action in their midst represented the earliest Bible. With the advent of writing and the use of papyrus, the sacred book came to be written and these experiences shared in more permanent form. The image of monks and other copiers spending their lives making copies of the Bible is one of the historic emblems of Christian dedication. Gutenberg's invention of movable type was a major assist to the Reformation's conviction of making the Bible available in their own tongue to the laity.

Translating the Bible is an important venture for the Christian community in every place and language where it exists. It is a labor of love as each word, phrase, chapter, and book is worked through from the original tongue to the contemporary one.

The translators of *The New English Bible* expressed this sense of agony and ecstasy:

The translators are as conscious as anyone can be of the limitations and imperfections of their work. No one who has not tried it can know how impossible an art translation is. Only those who have meditated long upon the Greek original are aware of the richness and subtlety of meaning that may lie even within the most apparently simple sentence, or know the despair that attends all efforts to bring it out through the medium of a different language.[1]

The Revised Standard Version of the Bible is a product of the support and imagination of the National Council of Churches of Christ in the USA and of a group of biblical scholars who have worked over two generations to produce a faithful translation and keep it up to date. A unique achievement, the RSV Bible is an authorized version for the Anglican, Orthodox, Protestant, and Roman Catholic traditions.

Biblical translation has never been an armchair venture. One is dealing here with holy writ, with people's images of meaning, and with the problem of translating from one language and culture to another. Questions have to be answered, such as: How can we be faithful to the original? How can we be clear in the current language? How can misconceptions be avoided because of cultural changes in word meaning? How can the cadence of the new language be established without destroying the literal meanings of the original?

In other eras, translators have been killed and their works destroyed. The Bible is a battleground for people and particular translations have been vilified by those whose views were offended by a particular version or verse. Bibles have been burned by the faithful as well as by the threatened state.

The struggle to secure a living Bible is and will be a continuing one. In our era, the National Council of Churches in the USA and its Revised Standard Version Bible Committee seek a revised translation that will take into account the concern for inclusive language about God and humans and address the cultural limitations that may reflect anti-Semitic, racially exclusive, or class expressions. The issue here is the ancient one — how to express the original intent in contemporary form.

A major struggle is going on over this issue. A Task Force on Biblical Translation was created by the National Council to explore the possibilities and limitations of providing a biblical text that uses inclusive language about God and humanity and avoids the limitations of racial or class perspectives. The task force made recommendations, which were subsequently adopted in two areas — work within the RSV committee and the preparation of experimental work for congregational use which would be based upon the RSV text but would seek more inclusive language for worship.

Every generation and every language community search to find the appropriate forms through which the eternal meanings of the Bible can be understood as "the Word of God for us today." Krister Stendahl, a New Testament teacher and former dean of Harvard Divinity School, expresses it this way:

Language is a living thing. Therefore, any reference to what Webster says or what the grammarians say, is partly beside the point. Language is in the making, and the task we are concerned with is not to just lock ourselves into specific suggestions as to translation, but to place ourselves on the spectrum of a living and evolving English language in, for, and out of the church and its perceptions. Although this sounds very general, it is important!

There is no doubt in my mind that we are at a point where, especially in terms of inclusive language, there is a new sensitivity, a new awareness, and there is no question that out of this will come a new language in the church. Constantly, when we discuss Bible translation, let us be aware of how poetry, liturgy, and hymns are written today. Some of the new words that have emerged out of a new consciousness, such as humankind for mankind, are in the process of becoming common language. Thus our task here is one both of translation and of aiding a new language to be born in the worshipping and total life of the church.[2]

News Release—National Council Gives Go-Ahead for Inclusive-Language Lectionary

NEW YORK, Nov. 26 — A division of the National Council of Churches has taken an important step toward developing nonsexist versions of Scripture, voting to prepare a collection of biblical passages for public worship that will minimize language that excludes women.

The council's Division of Education and Ministry will appoint a task force of writers and biblical scholars to adapt passages of the Revised Standard Version of the Bible. In the words of the division's proposal, the task force is to use "language which expresses inclusiveness with regard to human beings and which attempts to expand the range of images beyond the masculine to assist the Church in understanding the full nature of God."

"This task should be motivated," the division added, "by a pastoral regard for clear Christian witness in our period of cultural and religious history. It should be constrained by preserving the theological integrity of the biblical writers and by respecting the historic rootedness of their books."

The Scripture passages adapted will be those included in the three-year lectionary system used by many churches in their worship services. . .

The Division of Education and Ministry Committee, which includes representatives of most NCC member communions, voted to support continuation of the RSV Bible as a literal translation of the original Greek, Hebrew, and Aramaic manuscripts. The RSV Bible Committee, which is editorially independent, has indicated that it will use inclusive language only when such usage is consistent with the original texts.

The Division of Education and Ministry did vote, however, to request that "additional scholars with feminist perspectives become regular members of the RSV Bible Committee, as vacancies occur."

The effort to develop inclusive-language Scriptures came as a result of growing dissatisfaction among the NCC's member churches with biblical language that makes women appear secondary in the eyes of God or the Church. . .

The task force presented the option of new lectionary materials as a way to develop. . . [inclusive language] without jeopardizing the widespread acceptance of the RSV Bible. "On the one hand," it said, "the Revised Standard Version has become standard and normative to an extent that no other English translation has since the King James Version.

"This, of all translations, must not lend aid and comfort to sexist attitudes and interpretations. It should not disenfranchise half of humanity by being addressed to 'the brethren' alone. It should not speak of God or Christ in a manner that could make males feel superior and closer to God and Christ.

"On the other hand, many of us hesitate when it comes to such revisions of the Revised Standard Version, which could make it lose its distinction of being the standard translation through which our churches, seminaries, colleges, universities, and total culture have reasonable access to the language and conceptuality of the ages in which the biblical texts took shape. . ."

The task force gave some suggestions about the use of alternate language, such as:

substituting phrases such as "human beings" for "men;"

finding language about Jesus Christ to "overcome the undesired suggestions that the incarnation makes Christ's maleness crucial in such a way as to overshadow the primary import of the Word having become flesh, and the Divine having become human."

and minimizing references to God as "He" simply by refraining from the use of pronouns to describe God.

"Strictly and theologically speaking," the division said, "no statement about God as Lord, King, Father or He expresses a male reality set over against female reality. The sense of God as Father has no meaning of fatherhood as over/against motherhood.

"The question before us then is how to use our limited human language, and in our case, the specific limitations and possibilities of contemporary American English, in order to express this basic theological awareness."[3]

The NCCC Gets Letters...

August 11, 1981
To the Writers and
Biblical Scholars
National Council of Churches
475 Riverside Drive
New York, New York 10027

Gentlemen:
(this includes women)

A nonsexist Bible is nonescence [sic], because we have different sexes. Jesus, the Son of God, *was a male* and I don't believe God was ashamed to call him Son. Since we were made different, what's wrong with referring to the sex of a child?

Since Jesus referred to God as His Father, I choose to believe that He knew what He was talking about, and so should you. Even though God is our Source, Father implies much more.

Because men have failed so miserably as fathers (administrators of their families), women have rebelled — and rightly so. The better way is for you to teach man to know what God expects of him (how to protect his family, provide, and communicate with his wife, and how to properly discipline children without being abusive), and help him fulfill his God-given role, instead of changing what God has commissioned him to do.

You should be teaching us in a way that women won't feel inferior to men nor feel discriminated against because they don't do the same things. That's not where it's at. Jesus certainly treated men and women with same respect, even though they had different roles. That doesn't mean that God loves us less.

Women who know who they are spiritually and experience God's love and Presence feel secure and at peace and know they are loved.... They don't need to depend on feminine words to give them that assurance because they know they already have it in their hearts.

Because men have misinterpreted and misapplied God's laws is no reason to change the bible. Your job is to busy yourself telling us what conditions we must meet to receive God's love, forgiveness and how to let Him govern our lives, our human feelings and actions. Then you'll be rendering a better service to the Lord, with better results.

Praying for better
knowledge of His Word,

Lydia DiVito,
Bronx, New York[4]

Insights from Netherlands Churches

The rediscovery of the liberating power of the biblical writings is a central experience of people in the grass roots groups and critical communities. Many people find that their eyes are opened to the political and social dimensions of the biblical message by seeing injustice, oppression and social conflicts. Given this political broadening of awareness, new questions arise concerning church and faith...

God's choice of Israel is a choice of a slave people. It obliges them not to become oppressors, not to have gods as other people have them. If Israel degenerates into a kingdom based on might, this means incurring the accusation of dividing one class against another. Prophets arise, who denounce justice and proclaim that God wants this world completely changed. In this tradition stands Jesus of Nazareth, the man who humbled himself to be a slave, and who trod the path of solidarity right to the end, to the death by torture on the Cross. It is this man who is called "Son of God." The texts that speak of this, and that are written as an expression of resistance against the dominant religious and social system in Israel, can now be understood in their true meaning only within a new, contemporary practice of resistance....

From this basic stance of solidarity with all who are oppressed and belittled, key biblical words regain their original force. Two examples:

The key biblical word "reconciliation" is often used to deny or cover up conflicts and to banish all struggle, and thus class struggle too, as unchristian. Reconciliation, however, is far from meaning the abolition of all conflicts; it demands radical striving for a new social order—and that has to derive from "conversion," that is, complete change to new life.

The key biblical word "salvation," or "redemption," means an exodus in which all forms of injustice are left behind, as are all relationships whereby people are pressed into service and demeaned. The Bible must not be used to reinforce the oppression of the poor, of women, or black people, of Jews, of Palestinians, or of any other group of people. Every generation of Christians has the task of taking concrete steps, in the historical conditions in which they live, toward the "kingdom of God," the society wherein justice dwells. In this struggle for justice, Jesus became a "partisan for the poor."[5]

Throughout the world intentional communities of Christians meet for Bible study and Christian action. The Bible takes on fresh meanings for them as they struggle with its application to their own situation. These reflections come from groups of Christians in the Netherlands.

Prayer:

O God, the Parent of our Lord Jesus Christ, and our Parent, thou who art to us both Father and Mother: We who are thy children draw around thy lotus feet to worship thee. Thy compassion is as the fragrance of the lotus. Though thou art enthroned in the heavens, we may draw nigh to thee; for thy feet stand upon the earth where we humans dwell. Thy Son, our Lord, was man.

We see thy compassion in Jesus. He gives content to the Hindu name for thee—Siva, the Kindly One. He gives significance to the Muslim address of thee — Allah, the Merciful. He embodies in the Godhead what the Buddhist worships in the Buddha—compassion itself.

Thou God of all the world, let our history teach us that we belong to thee alone and that thou alone dost belong to us. And thou art enough, for in thee we sinners find sonship and daughterhood again — the one thing that we need most.

D.T. Niles[6]

7.
Education for Liberation and Community

One of the earliest magnets which drew Christians together in the modern ecumenical era was the Sunday School and the other educational programs of churches. Laity planned and celebrated together long before their denominations officially started talking to each other.

This effort of teachers and students together is sometimes called "grassroots ecumenism." It may be the kind that matters most.

This movement took on global dimensions beginning with a World Sunday School Convention in London in 1839 and it was succeeded by thirteen other conventions through the 1950s. This organized movement was one of the roots of the World Council of Christian Education, a formal organization which began in Rome in 1907. This legacy continues as part of the World Council of Churches.

The Christian education calling today takes on many forms and dimensions. As churches were the first patrons of the arts, so they were of education. Primary schools, colleges, universities, seminaries, and graduate schools around the world bear the marks of the church's concern and patronage.

Redefining Education Ecumenically
Canadian Christians call this report "An Affection for Diversity."

Having spent some time on the social context of the ecumenical reality in Canada, it is essential now that we say what we mean by ecumenism itself.

We accept the meaning pointed to by the Greek: "oikumene" means the whole inhabited world. Ecumenism embraces the faithful of all religious persuasions, believers and nonbelievers as well, indeed, every child of God in quest for ultimate meaning and goodness. Exclusivity and ecumenicity do not belong together. The goal of ecumenism is to achieve the unity of humankind, through developing an affection for diversity and through sharing deeply in the revelation of God through the ages. Faithfulness to one's own particular experience of revelation implies sharing it, in love with others, most of whom will have had a quite different experience. Such sharing requires disciplined intervention, something quite different from cultural invasion and interference in the lives of others.

Within the quest for the unity of humankind, we understand the unity of the Church to be a special responsibility, a primary obligation for Christian ecumenists. The unity of the Church can be, as it were, a sacrament of the unity of humankind, and the difficulty of achieving it in faithfulness is a precious source of realism, patience and humility as we yearn for the wider human unity.

Within this broad framework of understanding, conceived of as the goal of ecumenism, three major objectives may be identified for education ecumenically:

One: shared reflection and renewal (the cultivation, in faith, of the devotional life).

Two: shared service to others (the giving of oneself through caring).

Three: shared social action (the reconstruction of structures with hope and love).

It is inconceivable that education ecumenically can be achieved unless all three of these objectives are sought...[1]

When we use the phrase "ecumenical education" we are not thinking of a new type of Christian education which is "ecumenical" in opposition to education which is carried out in various churches. The churches still provide the primary context in which most Christian education is received. Rather, we seek to point to the obligation of our churches to education for life in the *oikumene* — for life in the world and in the ecumenical situation which is a part of the life of all our churches today.[2]

41

Why Does the Church Engage in Education?

The Joint Educational Development denominations developed a statement of educational intent some years ago to answer the above question. The statement says in part that the church engages in education:

as a continuing means of sharing the gospel and of helping persons to make their own responses of faith; to broaden and deepen their perceptions of God, other persons, social issues and structures, and the natural world; and to develop skills of ethical decision-making and responsible participation in shaping the future of the human community.

as a means of equipping persons to understand, to enter into, and to help develop the life and ministries of a contemporary community of faith, rooted in the Christian heritage and charged with mission...

as a means of helping persons achieve full humanness. This involves: a) a sense of individual dignity, capacity, and worth; b) interpersonal relationships of trust, freedom, and love; and c) a society that enhances freedom, justice and peace for all people.

as a means of effecting justice and reconciliation within and through all social structures and systems. Essential to accomplishing this intention is an understanding of the interdependence of all people and a willingness to act to change the present unjust distribution of power and economic resources in the world.[3]

The Uniqueness of Christian Education

When the ministries of the World Council of Christian Education and the World Council of Churches came together they did so upon the basis of a joint study of the educational task. The study said in part:

Education in a Christian perspective is an effort to open the mind to the depth dimension of the reality in which human life is set: its aim is to prepare persons for effective, life-long, loving, and God-fearing service.... The materials of education are not only convenient ways of relating many learners to few teachers; they are the means of discovering the interdependence of God's creatures as co-learners....

Educated persons are those whose eyes and ears, mind and heart have been opened to the surprising richness of surrounding reality; who understand adequately the human society in which they live and themselves in relation to it; who have acquired skills of learning and acting; who give service to others and accept it from them with grace; who render the adoration of worship to their Creator.

The realization of this high purpose of education is limited, as all human endeavours are. Education cannot open for societies an automatic gateway to Utopia or assure success for individuals. Nor does education under church auspices guarantee salvation. The Christian view of education recognizes the thwarting and corrupting presence of evil in individuals and communities. Evil is not a sum of defects and shortcomings to be brushed aside. An optimistic view . . . distorts educational goals and methods by failing to recognize, as the source of human conflicts and social disorganization, our alienation from God and therefore from our own true life.

The Christian message is one of hope and confidence: God has in Christ shown the way for us to turn towards the true source and meaning of our lives which are in God and in the neighbor God gives us. This confidence will set the goal of education as freedom: freedom not centered in the ego, nor in dogmatic or ideological schemes, but in openness to others. Thus education will be directed to enabling new generations to make their own contribution to an on-going human culture and to developing the capacity to live a personal life of self-criticism, flexibility of mind and continual learning in the midst of changing or unstable social patterns.[4]

The Christian Community, Sign of Liberation

The Christian community is placed in the human community to present the total message of Christ and to be a sign of God's liberating power.... The entire life of the Christian community is educative, and the quality of its worship and work as a whole determines the quality of the nurture of its members. Each local congregation is called to be a community, a *koinonia* which reflects the care and love of God for all people. In such a fellowship all members have their part and must contribute to the life of the whole. Christian education is a vital part of this, for it belongs to the whole church and is the responsibility of all its members....

At the center of the learning experience in the church stands worship and the liturgy. This is the joyous expression of the Christian's dependence on God and Christ's presence in the life of his community. We must constantly examine church practices to see if they divorce liturgy from life. The liturgy must lead us to participate in the fellowship of God and guide us to service and witness in and to the world.[5]

Fifth Assembly, World Council of Churches, 1975.

The Churches' Concern for Public Education

The churches singly and together have an historic concern for the quality and character of public education. The education provided in state-sponsored schools provides a meeting ground for people of all backgrounds. This concern was expressed in a pronouncement of the National Council of Churches in the U.S.A. Excerpts follow:

We affirm our support as a nation and as individuals and communities within the nation to the system of public schooling in the United States

recognizing that the "right to a free education" is one of the universally accepted basic rights;

recognizing that a free and public education is one of the success stories in the education of a people, and a significant piece of the American dream;

recognizing that education is a distinctive and priceless function of a society, and that public elementary and secondary schools are basic social and educating institutions in America;

recognizing that education is unmatched in the extent to which it enables the development of personality, character and the capability to participate in a pluralistic and democratic society, and, as such, the public schools are a major cohesive force in preparing all citizens for living in a diverse and interdependent world;

recognizing that while families have the right to choose nonpublic or religiously affiliated schools, and that many such nonpublic schools are commendable in the extent to which they serve a public function at private expense, nonetheless, the public schools, being the primary vehicles for equality of educational opportunity in our society, are the responsibility of all citizens, financially and through involvement, creativity and struggle:

We commit ourselves to assume a more active role in applying gospel principles of justice and human fulfillment to the issues facing public schools in our community.[6]

A Litany of Education and Community

Leader: The old order is passing away; your new order, Lord, has already begun and we are numbered among its signs. Through your Spirit in our hearts you have set us free.

People: Give us insight and courage to follow where you lead us.

Leader: You have opened our eyes, given us hope that we shall live in the glorious liberty of the children of God. . . But not alone, Lord; not while others remain poor, broken-hearted, imprisoned, blind and bruised. Yet. . .

People: Give us insight and courage to follow where you lead us.

Leader: So, Lord, we pray for our brothers and sisters, your family, oppressed by ignorance and poverty, caught in a web of injustice and apathy, cut off from one another by language, culture, colour, class and creed.

People: Give us insight and courage to follow where you lead us.

Leader: Through education may the powerless be led to self-discovery, the despised find new dignity, the dispossed be enabled to claim their place in the community of free people.

People: Give us insight and courage to follow where you lead us.

Leader: Give to your church a vision of the total liberation of humanity.
Grant us the wisdom to hear the voice of the foolish of the world, the strength to listen to the weak, that through those who are nothing we may understand the word of Christ.

People: Give us insight and courage to follow where you lead us.

Leader: But we tend to love darkness rather than light. We shrink from the responsibility of freedom, the uncertainty of the desert, the conflict of the cross. We keep turning back, preferring the security of slavery to the adventure of the promised land.

People: Call us out of darkness into your marvellous light.

Leader: Call us, Lord Jesus Christ, that we may follow. May we follow you not only as one who goes ahead but as one who journeys with us: Lord Jesus Christ, freeing us, uniting us! Let us be content to learn the meaning of your Way as we walk in it.

Amen.[7]

8.
Through the Artists' Perceptions

Artists express the meaning of life and faith through their media. Grant Spradling states it this way:

The arts are a slender, fragile answer to the human creature's esthetic longing. The aching of the eye to see more deeply, the ear to be thrilled, to experience tantalizing touch and smell, to consume and be consumed in that reality within which each creature lives—those longings of the soul are never fully assuaged by a work of art. Yet, the arts are the most pervasive outcropping of the human capacity to participate in reality through the senses.

God is the original artisan, creating shape, form, and purpose, giving life, and establishing the possibility of continuing creativity. Being created in God's image involves the talent for conceptualization, creative form, and aesthetic appreciation.[1]

Throughout the ages the faith community has been a patron of the arts and artists. David danced before the Ark. Psalm 150 is a high note of praise. Synagogue, temple, altar and church have continually expressed both the artists' and the congregations' senses of holy space. Much of the great music, poetry, dance, sculpture, and theatre represent a religious offering. Much of it explores biblical themes and/or biblical meanings.

There is another strand in the Hebrew-Christian tradition that reflects the commandment against creating graven images and worries about idolatry. This was expressed particularly in the Puritan tradition. In fact, the early Puritan settlers in the New World forbade the celebration of Christmas because they felt it led in the direction of idolatry. The church, too, has had almost a fetish about the spoken and the literary word to the detriment of other forms of expression and communication.

In a word, the church, the arts and the artists have struggled with each other to find an authentic relationship. Churches together in various ecumenical forms continue that struggle.

The Church and the Arts

The relationship of the church and the arts takes many forms. One of them is the concern for church space and form. Church architecture, building, grounds and appointments reflect the faith statements of congregations expressed by artisans in concrete forms.

A second area is that of liturgy. Music, dance, spoken word, symbol, sacrament and movement are aesthetic forms through which faith is conveyed to and through the senses. Carla de Sola reflects this as she speaks of movement in liturgy:

I pray that everyone, sitting cramped inside a pew, body lifeless, spine sagging and suffering, weary with weight and deadness, will be given space in which to breathe and move, will be wooed to worship with beauty and stillness, song and dance—dance charged with life, dance that lifts up both body and spirit, and we will be a holy, dancing, loving, praying and praising people.[2]

The church continues its patronage of the arts in a variety of ways. Works of art are commissioned and displayed. Arts festivals are sponsored giving artists a chance to share their gifts and sell their creations. The World Council of Churches is engaged in serious dialogue with artists, especially in Third World countries. This grows out of an awareness of the crucial role of the artist in shaping the images and possibilities of the life of new nations.

Hillcrest United Church of Christ in Whittier, California, has sponsored a community arts festival each year for many years. More than 20,000 people attend and artists participate by invitation. This is a judged exhibition. Senior Pastor Ted Robinson interprets the church's rationale:

It is part of the mission of the church to bring creative fulfillment, festivity, and beauty into human lives. It is natural that the church should be involved in the arts. Not only are the arts an integral part of the life of the church as seen in architecture, song, and the spoken word, but both religion and art tend to draw upon many of the same insights for their expression.

We are living in a time of great interest in the arts. It is valuable, not only for its beauty but also as an expression of the culture in which we live. It represents

47

much work, thought, emotion and symbolism. The paintings you see about you, the musician playing classical music on the organ, the potter forming clay into an object both useful and beautiful, the actor sharing a message, and all the other art forms, represent expression of the present and the heritage of which we are a part.[3]

An Old Union

Probably no union since Adam and Eve is as old and prolific as that of religion and art. Greek drama, African sculpture, Byzantine painting, Medieval architecture, the Classical dance of India, the music of the Church—the list is endless. So deeply intertwined are the origins of religion and the arts that they seem to be analytically indistinguishable.

That so symbiotic a relationship should exist for so long is not hard to understand. Religion and the arts share a sense of awe before the mysteries of life. They share a profound sense of ritual, of ceremony and celebration. The devotion of artists to their work is not dissimilar from that of clerics to their vocation.[4]

Livingston Biddle
National Endowment on the Arts

Imaging Life

The arts are not for the privileged few, but for the many. Their place is not on the periphery of daily life, but at its center. They should function not merely as another form of entertainment, but, rather, should contribute significantly to our well being and happiness.[5]

John D. Rockefeller III

The arts always speak of things absent, where dreams are formed. As problem solvers we have been so preoccupied with immediate causes that we appear incapable of dreaming a new world into existence. Our concern for ethics has preoccupied us with the observance of the rules so that we have ignored the aesthetics out of which new rules are created. Indeed, aesthetics are the ethics of the future.[6]

Wesley A. Hotchkiss

All Christian art can only point to the true image of God which became manifest in Jesus Christ. . . Yet there is a more existential way of making that image visible—by ourselves being transfigured into this "icon" of God which appeared in Christ, as the apostle Paul once wrote to the Corinthians (II Corinthians 3:18). The church itself is called to become God's artwork and the life of Christians is meant to be the continuous interpretation of the life, death and resurrection of Christ.[7]

Hans-Ruedi Weber

The Arts, The Public and the Churches

The churches together are concerned for public support of artists and of the arts. The Montana Association of Churches sponsored a town meeting on the arts. One of the products of this continuing emphasis within the association is focus upon public funding. The position statement in part says:

The Montana Association of Churches supports:

Full access to the arts by all Montanans in their schools, communities and public institutions;

increased state support for the arts, realizing that the ideal system of support for the arts in a free society is a combination of public, private and corporate money;

the development of economic and social policies which will encourage the arts as a way of life and enable artists to live and work in Montana.

The Church throughout the ages has been a patron and preserver of the arts and the artists, and thus it is not an unusual stance for churches to take today. Moreover, churches are recognizing the development of the whole person as a cultural, social, political and spiritual being, a part of which is the potential for magnificent creative activity within each of us as we respond to the creator God.

Who has a right to make art, who has access to artistic experiences, who has a right to an esthetically rich life, and even who may define what art is—these are questions which must be answered with the broadest possible audience in mind. . . . The quality of life within our communities can be measured by the opportunities to enjoy and participate in the arts by all persons.

Montana is at the bottom of the list of states in legislative appropriation to the arts. In the last decade, the unique combination of public and private funding which has nurtured the growth of the arts has made a strong philosophical statement that the arts are as vital to our lives as food and work. It has also had the practical result of unprecedented growth in business support of the arts. Private philanthropy has sustained much of our cultural treasure, but it is usually not willing to take the risks of funding art on the growing edge, nor in developing programs in profitably unstable areas. . . .

We support and encourage the arts as a way of making a living in Montana. As public funding and public policies support the arts as a priority,. . . . the artist will find Montana an economically viable place in which to work. The arts are good business—high value, self-employed, labor intensive, clean, good for communities—and have a real economic impact on an area.[8]

Dedication

I will send my poems flying
in unyielding defiance
against a system
which forever puts property
ahead of people.

I will send my poems flying
against the multi-national corporations
which exploit and brutally repress
millions of Latin Americans and Asians
and throw thousands of U.S. citizens
out of work
for the sake of their profits.

I will send my poems flying
against a culture
which permits its senior citizens
to live out their last years
neglected and impoverished.

I will send my poems flying
against a society
which places good education and health care
out of reach of millions of children
whose parents are too exhausted
from their daily struggle for survival
to guide and enjoy them.

I will send my poems flying,
I refuse to accept
that my Black and Native American
sisters and brothers
must live stunted, shortened lives
in blighted, crime-ridden ghettos.

I will send my poems flying,
no longer will I be manipulated
by the televised purveyors
of detergents and deodorants.

I will send my poems flying,
perhaps somewhere, someone
who can make a difference
will read them.[9]

Mary Jane Brewster

A Litany of Praise and Celebration

This delightful litany was part of the festival of choirs at First Presbyterian Church in Orange, California

Leader: O God of the circus and God of the game, God of the market-place and God of the street,
People: God of the school and God of politics, God of the hospital and God of the factory,
Leader: God of the farm and God of the city park, God of the airport and God of the pier,
People: God of the publishing house and God of the TV station, God of heaven and God of earth,
Leader: God of Jesus and God of the Church.
All: O God of everything and everyone, Hear our prayer of praise![10]

9.
Faith, Science and Technology

Christians live together in an age with rapidly expanding knowledge. In the realm of science this has led to better understanding of the processes of life itself, nutrition, health, food production, and the universe. Technology—from computers to communications to space shuttles—is transforming life in the workplace, at home, at leisure, and in military affairs. The pursuits of science and technology raise frightening concerns in such fields as biology, weaponry and energy.

Increasingly Christians, scientists and technologists (often one and the same person) are looking afresh at issues of faith, science and technology. In doing so, the practices, products, benefits, and liabilities of these efforts are brought under scrutiny.

Alfred North Whitehead in 1926 looked at these relationships and penned this prophetic statement, "When we consider what religion is for humankind, and what science is, it is no exaggeration to say that the future course of history depends upon the decision of this generation as to the relations between them."[1]

Science and the Modern World was Whitehead's popular statement of the relation of religion and science. His emphasis upon processes in science and in religion provided common ground for the two disciplines. Churches and church leaders ever since have sought to understand the linkages, insights and differences between the two ways of perceiving reality.

Scientist Charles Birch electrified the Nairobi Assembly of the World Council of Churches in 1975 with his statements on the relation of faith and environment. For example:

Each person born on earth has a negative impact on the environment. An Australian or an American has a much larger impact than a Kenyan or an Indonesian, perhaps twenty times as much. The total negative impact of all the people on earth is, in its simplest terms, a product of three items. The equation is as follows: total population times consumption of resources per person equals environmental deterioration per person. The more the people, the more the impact, the more environmental deterioration, the greater the impact. Every item in the equation is increasing. Population will double in thirty-five years. Energy use has doubled in ten years. Pollution has doubled in fourteen years. The result is a steadily multiplying impact of every human being on the environment which cannot continue without the gravest consequences for humanity and the rest of creation.[2]

From the biblical perspective, human well-being depends upon our living in faithful obedience to God within the limits our Creator determines for us. Science, assisted by technology, as our way of knowing the natural and social dimensions of our existence, makes it possible for us to act with understanding towards each other and our environment. Faith provides us with the spiritual and moral values which should guide and regulate our application of science and technology. To gain an understanding and an appreciation of the mysteries of creation reverently fulfills the human spirit. To use this understanding irresponsibly leads to great suffering, destruction and the brutalization of both those who wield the power and those against whom it is directed.[3]

Race Toward Catastrophe

It is the considered views of many scientists and technologists that the world is on a catastrophic course leading to mass starvation, global depletion of resources, and global environmental deterioration. The responsibility that now confronts humanity is to make a deliberate transition to a sustainable global society in which science and technology will be mobilized to meet the basic physical and spiritual needs of people, minimize human suffering, and to create an environment that can sustain a decent quality of life of all people. This will involve a radical transformation of civilization, new technologies, new uses for technology, and new global economic and political systems.[4]

Churches should foster a heightened moral awareness among their members engaged in

53

scientific and technological activities. They themselves should participate in and should promote representative participation in the discussion of ethical issues raised by technologies and their implementation. The churches and their members should call in question immoral or amoral behaviour in scientific or technological activities. This questioning is a continuation of the traditional prophetic role of the Church in society.[5]

It is God whom Job questioned. Did God then vouchsafe to him a revelation to solve the mystery that so oppressed him? In the reply of Yahweh there is nothing but an injunction to open his eyes and look abroad over the grandeur and mystery of the universe. . .

And Yahweh said to Job:
"Who is this obscuring my
    designs
with his empty-headed words?
Brace yourself like fighter;
now it is my turn to ask
    questions and you to inform
    me,
Where were you when I laid
    the foundations of the earth?
Tell me, since you are so
    well-informed!
Who decided the dimensions of
    it, do you know?. . .
Have you journeyed all the
    ways to the sources of the
    sea,
or walked where the Abyss is
    deepest?
Have you been shown the gates
    of Death
or met with the janitors of
    Shadowland?
Have you an inkling of the
    extent of the earth?
tell me about it if you
    have!. . .
    Job 38. The Jerusalem Bible

Some of these questions are questions to us, though not all. . . . We have journeyed all the way to the sources of the sea and beyond to the moon. We have walked where the abyss of the sea is deepest and now we plan to dig it up. We think we know something about the beginnings of the universe and the beginnings of life. But our dominant scientific technological worldview and a good deal of the Christian theology that accompanies it provides no framework within which we can find comprehensible answers to questions of point and purpose.

What, then, might Yahweh say to the modern questioner?

Who is this obscuring my designs with his mechanistic models of the universe so that there is room neither for purpose, mind or consciousness?

Brace yourself like a fighter, for now it is my turn to ask questions and yours to inform me.

Where were you at the Big Bang?

How is it that out of a universe of pure hydrogen you have come into existence?

Did life begin when the first cell came into existence or do elements of life exist in the foundations of the universe?

How can you be so sure that all is contrivance? How can mind grow from no mind? How can life grow from the non-living?

Do people grow from blind mechanism? Is not a universe which grows human beings as much a human or humanizing universe as a tree which grows apples is an apple tree?

Or do you think that figs grow on thistles and grapes on thorns?

Does the life of Jesus not tell you something about the life of the universe? Was he not there in some sense from the foundations of it all?

You who live in rich countries, can you not see how every increase in your standard of living reduces that of someone in a poor country as well as threatening the survival of future generations? Who is madly Christian enough among you to cut his standard of living by a third for the sake of the poor?

Do you think that the world and all that is in it is simply for your use? Has it no other value?

Because there are accidents and chance in the world, why do you think there is therefore no room for purpose? Can you not have both?

And when you have analyzed life down to its molecular building blocks in DNA, why do you think you have discovered the secret of life when you have not yet discovered the source of love and all feeling?

And why do you want to make of me either an all-powerful engineer or an impotent non-entity when I am neither?

To all of this we can only reply as Job replied:

"I have been holding forth on
  matters I cannot understand
on marvels beyond me and my
  knowledge.
I knew you then only by
  hearsay;
but now, having seen you with
  my own eyes,
I retract all I have said, and in
  dust and ashes I repent."

Job 42

That is an encounter of the ultimate kind. Intelligence is almost useless to those who possess nothing else. Confession of incompetence, according to the book of Job, is the beginning of wisdom.[6]

10.
JPSS–A Slogan or a Passion?

Across the broad ecumenical horizon a vision emerges, haunted by the spectre of its opposite. It is labelled JPSS—for Just, Participatory, and Sustainable Society. It is an appropriate energizing passion for the churches in their life together.

Our Lord said, "I am come that they may have life and have it abundantly." JPSS is today's form of defining that life for society.

Justice has to do with valuing each human being and supporting that person's right to an equitable share of the earth's resources and protection from threats to life, growth, and personhood. It includes a political, economic, and social arrangment of things which is just. The right to redress grievances is also included.

Participatory refers to the potential involvement of each person in shaping the events and affairs which impact his or her life. Whatever the structures or forms of goverance, the notion is one of a voice and a share in the power.

Sustainable refers to the use and limits of the earth's resources. Certain physical and economic resources undergird any society's daily life. Decisions about those resources today impact generations to come.

These three elements are interdependent. A totalitarian society that may be sustainable is neither just nor participatory. A participatory society that ignores justice and sustainability is inadequate. A just society, however participatory, that does not have the physical and economic resources to endure is doomed.

The spectre of the opposite vision is all too present in our world. Human rights are violated. The structures of injustice predominate. The majority of the world's peoples have little say in the issues that affect their destiny and that of their children. The present abuse and expenditure of the world's capital resources in relation to population raise grave questions about a sustainable future.

Thus, the importance of the vision. "Where there is no vision, the people perish."

The cry of liberation of this people is a clamor that ascends to God and that nothing nor no one can stop.

Archbishop Oscar A. Romero
El Salvador, 1980

Give Us This Day Our Daily Bread

The cause which claims us is the effort to secure bread and justice for all members of the human family. It can be expressed in various ways.

Put most simply, our cause is *to reduce needless human misery*. We are convinced that much of the suffering endured by hundreds of millions of our neighbors who live in absolute poverty and suffer chronic malnutrition is needless. This massive human misery is not the fruit of the strange working of fate; it is a function of the way society is structured. It is not a consequence of an insufficiency of resources; it is a result of the maldistribution of resources—and of the power to decide how resources shall be distributed. . . .

Expressed another way, our cause is *to seek universal respect for human dignity and human rights*. All persons hold certain rights. . . . To be respected as a person is a human right. To be treated fairly is another. To be

spared needless suffering is another. To have access to food is another. . . .

This means, finally, that our cause is *to help fashion a more just society*. A just society is one ordered in such a way that every person receives what she or he is entitled to. And what is every person's due? That she or he be treated according to the full stature of her or his humanity. . . .

We are aware that the fashioning of a more just society will require more than new government policies and new social, economic, and political structures. It will require new visions, new loyalties, new attitudes, new ways to seeing things. . . . We intend to work with others inside and outside the religious community in the search for a new social vision and the development of a new ethic of global solidarity. But our immediate task, in faithfulness to the cause, is to seek to influence and help others influence the shape of our

57

government's policy so that the United States will help rather than hinder the emergence on a global and international levels of a just, participatory, and sustainable society.[1]

The Interreligious Task Force
on U.S. Food Policy

Justice

Justice is a central focus of the Judeo-Christian tradition. The Old Testament alone has 116 references to justice. In addition, there are several dozen references each to judge, judged, judgment, and just. Connections with the doctrine of atonement and with the calling to righteousness are strong links with the justice theme.

In the biblical tradition, justice is one of the attributes of God. The problem of evil becomes so complex because the Bible assumes that God is just and, therefore, the question of why evil exists must be faced.

"Righteousness and justice" are said to be "the foundation of [God's] throne." (Psalm 89:14) "What does the Lord require of you," asks Micah (6:8), "but to do justice. . ."

According to Amos, God rejects solemn assemblies and offerings, preferring that "justice roll down like waters, and righteousness like an ever flowing stream."

When Matthew interprets Jesus' sense of calling in the twelfth chapter, he explains Jesus' sense of vocation by quoting Isaiah 42:1–4, which describes God's servant as one who "shall proclaim justice to the Gentiles" and "who brings justice to victory." Jesus stresses the obligation to justice in Matthew 23:23.

If the world were a global village of one hundred people, seventy of them would be unable to read, and only one would have a college education. Over 50 would be suffering from malnutrition, and over 80 would live in what we call substandard housing. If the world were a global village of 100 residents, 6 of them would be wealthy. These 6 would have half of the village's entire income, and the other 94 would exist on the other half.[2]

It is the duty of every person and every society to recognize that resources are limited. Further, it is a clear implication of the Christian understanding of the activity of God in creation, that all men and women are to benefit from it and that every person has the same right to use these resources responsibly. Hence no individual or group should be excluded from sharing in them or deciding how they should be used. When resources are scarce, the justice of the market system is most questionable, since it eliminates those who cannot afford the price from benefitting.

Clearly different resources raise the need for different criteria in their distribution, since the needs of individuals and societies will differ. However, it is too easy for both individuals and societies to translate a "want" into a "need." When this happens, the unjustifiable wants of one community may deny another community its justifiable needs. As a Christian community we must become more aware of this issue and must attempt some definition of "wants" and "need" in the wider context of understanding what it is to be human. A just society will attend to needs before it turns to the satisfaction of mere wants. Yet it will recognize that needs are not for mere physical subsistence, but include the expression of the gifts of artistic creation and imagination.[3]

Canadian Ten Days for World Development

Clear-headed and effective action which promotes social justice and human development is often made difficult in programs concerning global problems because of a fuzzy understanding of precisely what is helpful to the Third World and what it is possible to motivate people to do.

Sometimes education programs about Third World problems insist upon constantly speaking about faraway countries and peoples. This is fine if the goal is to raise funds to send support overseas. Refugee programs focus on the plight of peoples far away and then bring home opportunities for specific action here.

Issues such as bank loans to South Africa, or Nestle's and infant formula promotion necessarity combine information about South Africa and Third World countries with an emphasis on Canadian banking practices and the call for a North American consumer boycott of Nestle's, to cite just two examples. . . .

Canada cannot effectively promote justice internationally if we as a country are not "justice people" with "justice policies." This means that Canada must itself become a "just, participatory and sustainable society," no longer controlled by a small economic elite and emasculated by transnational corporations. Every day our export policies, our natural resource extraction policies, debt structure, profit maximization concerns, all send messages to the Third World about what we think development is.[4]

Che Jesus—A Prayer

(Che *is an Argentine salutation that has no precise English equivalent. The word is used by good friends in a common cause and implies friendship, commitment, and solidarity. This prayer was part of an anonymous leaflet in an industrial neighborhood in Cordoba, Argentina, in the 1970 Christmas season.)*

Che Jesus,
They told me that you came back to be born every Christmas.
Man, you're crazy!
Two thousand years ago you came and we nailed you to a tree, but
  you insist. . .
Don't you realize that every day we continue to crucify you?
After all, weren't you the one who said, "Whatever you do to any of
  those poor ones you do it to me?"
And can't you see what we are doing to you?

Every time a businessman exploits or deceives a worker,
Every time that a labor leader deceives or sells out his companions,
Every time that a professional profits from the misfortune of another
  human being,
Every time a merchant robs or a husband is unfaithful to his wife,
When an employee looks down on his fellow workers and draws a
  line separating those who wear ties from those who don't,
When a worker wishes to become bourgeois, seeking his own gain
  and his own promotion, not thinking of others and not feeling
  responsible for the liberation of all people.

And that's not all, Che Jesus. And when do we, together, kill you?

When one people enslaves another,
When we wage war on other nations because we have to sustain this
  rotten consumer society which we ourselves invented,
When we let the wise guys fill our homes with the trash from a
  television set which has our children hypnotized,
When we do not denounce injustice nor relate to the struggle against
  the exploitation, the backwardness
-The causes which so neatly impede the progress of the people.

And yet, you want to come anyway?
I don't know what with this stubborn gesture of coming back every
  Christmas you are trying to tell us something.

That the revolution that all proclaim begins first of all in each one's
heart,
That it doesn't mean only changing structures but changing selfish-
ness for love,
That we have to stop being wolves and return to being brothers and
sisters,
That we stop losing time in criticizing and begin to work seriously for
individual conversion and social change that will give to all the
possibility of having bread, education, freedom, and dignity.
That you have a message that's called the Gospel,
And a Church, and that's us—
A Church that wants to be servant of all,
A Church that knows that because God became human one Christmas
there is no other way to love God but to love all people.
If that's the way it is, Jesus, come to my house this Christmas
Come to my country,
Come to the world of men and women.
And first of all, come to my heart.[5]

11.
Blessed Are the Peacemakers

Through its long history the Christian church has had the visions of a creation fashioned by God as a gift to all peoples, of the peaceable kingdom, and of Jesus the peacemaker. In season and out, the making of peace has been our calling.

The Christian church is a transnational and global enterprise. By definition, Christians are citizens of two realms seeking to reconcile both and to bring their vocation of peacemaker to their public citizenship.

The World Council of Churches could not have its formative meeting for long years because of the claims of World War II. The first assembly in Amsterdam in 1948 declared:

The churches must also attack the causes of war by promoting peaceful change and the pursuit of justice. They must stand for the maintenance of good faith and the honoring of pledged word, resist the pretentions of imperialism, promote the multilateral reduction of armaments, and combat indifference and despair in the face of the futility of war; they must point Christians to that spiritual resistance which, grown from settled convictions widely held, is itself a powerful deterrent to war.[1]

Swords into Plowshares

General Secretary Philip Potter of the World Council of Churches addressed the special session of the United Nations on disarmament in June of 1978. He said in part:

In face of this catalogue of accelerated insecurity, the churches cannot remain spectators and inactive. On the basis of their faith in a God who in Jesus Christ wills that we should have life and have it in all its fulness, and in

. . .[God's] purpose that the earth should be replenished and used for the well-being of all. Christians are called to bring new perspectives to bear on the issues of militarism and the arms race.[2]

Philip Potter then named four perspectives for Christians in dealing with this issue locally and globally:

1. Disarmament is an integral part of the struggle for a just, participatory, and sustainable society.

2. We must challenge the idol of a distorted concept of national security which is directed to encouraging fear and mistrust resulting in greater insecurity.

3. Christians are pledged to work for creating those structures and mechanisms by which disarmament can be sought boldly and imaginatively.

4. Disarmament is not the affair of statesmen and experts only, but of every man and woman of every nation.

The churches do not approach their task with any self-righteousness or naiveté. They are well aware that throughout their history they have often been so allied to the forces of disorder and oppression that they have promoted or connived in wars and in war psychosis. They know that their own divisions are symptoms and signs of the divisions in our world. To be instruments of reconciliation they are in fact endeavoring to become reconciled to each other.

It is in humility and hope that the churches participate in the efforts towards disarmament and a just society. They do so with the vision of the prophet, whose words are engraved on the Isaiah Wall just across the street from this building:

They shall beat their swords
  into plowshares and their
  spears into pruninghooks;
Nation shall not lift up sword
  against nation, neither shall
  they learn war any more.

It is this vision of the conversion of the tools of death into the tools of life which inspires and activates the churches today. Our prayer is that this vision will inspire you in your deliberations and your peoples in the pursuit of peace and justice.[3]

Toward a Bilateral Nuclear Freeze

WHEREAS the horror of a nuclear holocaust is universally acknowledged; and

WHEREAS today the United States and the Soviet Union possess 50,000 nuclear weapons; and

WHEREAS in half an hour, all cities in the northern hemisphere can be destroyed; and

WHEREAS over the next decade the USA and USSR plan to build over 20,000 more nuclear warheads, along with a new "generation" of missiles to deliver them long range;

WHEREAS the ratification of SALT II has been postponed and other arms control measures left in abeyance;

THEREFORE BE IT RESOLVED THAT THE BOARD OF DIRECTORS OF THE CHURCH COUNCIL OF GREATER SEATTLE JOINS WITH OTHER ORGANIZATIONS AND INDIVIDUALS IN CALLING FOR A BILATERAL NUCLEAR WEAPONS FREEZE, TO WIT:

The United States and the Soviet Union should immediately and jointly stop the nuclear arms race. Specifically, they should adopt an immediate, mutual freeze on all further testing, production and deployment of nuclear weapons and of missiles and new aricraft designed primarily to deliver nuclear weapons.[4]

May 1981

The Council of Churches of Greater Seattle like many local ecumenical structures is actively involved in applying the gospel to issues in the human community—local, national, and global.

A Prayer for Peace

Lord, make us instruments of your peace.
 Where there is hatred, let us sow love;
 where there is injury, pardon;
 where there is discord, union;
 where there is doubt, faith;
 where there is despair, hope;
 where there is darkness, light;
 where there is sadness, joy.
Grant that we may not seek so much to be comforted
 as to comfort;
 to be understood as to understand;
 to be loved as to love;
 for it is in giving that we receive;
 it is in forgiving that we are forgiven,
 and it is in dying that we are born into
 eternal life; through Jesus Christ our Lord.

St. Francis of Assisi[5]

12.
Social Responsibility in Investments

North American churches and church bodies have for many years invested funds (especially pension funds) in business corporations through the purchase of stocks and bonds. That makes them partial owners of these companies and in that sense responsible for products and actions.

Over the last fifteen years church bodies have become increasingly sophisticated in their ability to raise questions of employment practices, relationships with repressive governments, ecological issues, and ethical stances. Initial challenges came in the equal employment and racism areas and now reach into concern about the weapons of war and questions of the long-term survival of the human race. The role of multinational corporations and banks in South Africa has been a perennial concern as foreign capital has helped to shore up the structure of apartheid through which the white minority keeps in servitude the black and colored majority.

The Canadian task force is typical of many groups of Christians addressing the role of businesses and banks in supporting unjust structures or questionable policies.

The members of the [Task Force on the Churches and Corporate Responsibility] . . . have committed themselves to respond to the needs of sister churches working with disadvantaged groups, wherever the decisions of Canadian banks and corporations have an adverse effect on people who have no power to affect those decisions themselves. The Task Force takes action whenever there are serious violations of human, political or economic rights, and when those violations seem related to the presence of Canadian corporations.

In raising questions of the social impact of business decisions with Canadian corporations and government, the churches speak as shareholders, but also as major institutions in the country. They are themselves struggling to change their own behavior to reflect "God's preferential option for the poor." Therefore, they are painfully aware that they often find themselves living in a glass house, but they are also mindful of the fact that justice cannot be delayed until each of us has reached perfection.

The Task Force agenda has been dominated by international concerns, in part, because people living under oppressive regimes have few or no channels for redressing the wrongs they suffer. Neither do they have social cushions that we have built into our own society to protect ourselves from adverse social and economic hardships, such as unemployment insurance, health care, and welfare. In such situations, those who live closest to the breadline are the most exposed and vulnerable to the vagaries of political and economic power.

Hence, the commitment of the Canadian churches to magnify the voices of those who suffer. Where the poor cannot speak for themselves, the churches have undertaken to work in partnership with sister churches in making those voices heard.[1]

Annual Report of the Task Force on the Churches and Corporate Responsibility, Toronto

United Methodist Statement

As Christian people and inheritors of the covenant of Israel, we are called to be a community of priests (to one another) whose essential being in the world is to share God's love with all persons. This involves the assumption of the role of mediator—one who is the go-between with God and those who would be in relationship to God. This witness reveals that every person is priest to one's neighbor. Such a priestly perspective affords a radically different worldview, which has been reflected vividly through a model of caring and compassion dramatically exemplified by Jesus Christ.

The United Methodist Church has accepted its priestly role and has declared its accountability for the natural world as well as concern for the nurturing, social, economic, political, and world communities. The church has continually affirmed its historic mission in care for "the world as our parish" and in celebration of its Christian experience and witness.

Because of these commitments to become God's faithful witnesses in the world, United Methodists have sought to exercise their responsibility to improve the quality of the secular society. Thus the church has taken forthright and continued stands in opposition to the slave trade, mistreatment of minorities, liquor traffic, gambling, war, nuclear proliferation, unfair labor practices, consumer exploitation, environmental waste, and pollution, and policies that deny basic human rights.

In the continuing struggle to assert God's participation in human history, the church as a community of the reconciled has by resolution, and by actions, reminded the corporate and public business enterprise of its responsibility to engage in economic activity which enhances human dignity and the quality of life for consumers and citizens.[2]

A Scenario of the Future

The year was 1988. The place, Canada. It became known as the year in which Canadian Christians finally came of age. The line was now clear between those who had chosen a "negative peace which is the absence of tension," and those who had chosen "a positive peace which is the presence of justice." It was the year many Christians began to use their critical consciousness to see their value systems not as self-evident truths about what models for society were best but as working hypotheses which must be continually modified through action and reflection.

It was the year in which the need to be in conflict was fully accepted as a necessary means to reach genuine reconciliation. So greatly had society changed since the late 1970s that the fear of taking sides and working with some people *against* others in the struggle for justice on a particular issue disappeared. . . .

Looking now at the new political party, Justice First, with its 34 seats in the House of Commons, created by the efforts of church, labour, native people, environmentalists, and hundreds of Canadians from all walks of life, a whole new approach to our economy and our understanding of unemployment nationally and internationally–I can scarcely believe all this happened in only nine short years.

Across the country you find major progress being made in the cooperative movement and in worker control experiments. We have learned much from the efforts of the Third World societies and now also share the experience of our efforts with them. Great strides are being made with more decentralized units of production and with greater participation by those who work in them.

Not all is going well. Indeed our world seems to have more conflicts in it now than in the past twenty years. . . . Events on the world stage moved very quickly. The struggle to end apartheid in

South Africa reached a decisive stage. The massive revolutionary struggles which blew up in Latin America were responded to by direct military intervention by the U.S.A. when popular uprising began in Brazil. This caused the U.S.A. to put enormous pressure on Canada for energy supplies. But for the first time. . . Canada refused to export more energy to the U.S. With multinationals moving out of Canada to take advantage of lower wages in Asia and new markets in China, it is understandable that the 21% unemployment rate across Canada had a radicalizing effect.

There are now clear lines of division between "status quo Christians" and the "Christians for justice" still struggling within the churches. Similar lines developed between labour groups caused I think by a split between those who wanted to give in to U.S. pressure and those who wanted to re-structure our society along the lines of the World Council of Churches' "just, participatory and sustainable society. . ."

I look back and wonder what effect our Ten Days for World Development program had in any of this new thinking—I wonder if we could have been able to influence the whole question of Canada's policies toward international development and unemployment if we had not begun that critical church/workers dialogue back in 1979.

It is clear that more and more people around the world and in Canada are committed to the reconciliation which grows out of the inevitable conflicts in the struggle for justice. I wonder if Ten Days contributed in any small way to this global process. What did we do right then?[3]

O God, who has bound us together in this bundle of life, give us grace to understand how our lives depend upon the courage, the industry, the honesty and the integrity of our fellows . . . that we may be mindful of their needs, grateful for their faithfulness, and faithful in our responsibilities to them; through Jesus Christ our Lord. Amen[4]

Reinhold Niebuhr

13.
In Pursuit of Human Rights

The United Nations Declaration of Human Rights came into being because nation-states in their best moments recognized the right of all human beings to a social context in which their humanity could flourish. Christians take their cue from Jesus, who declared, "I am come that they may have life and have it abundantly."

The ecumenical community has sought to enlarge both the concept and the practice of human rights. That involves actions directed toward particular governments, such as South Africa, South Korea, El Salvador, Chile, Bolivia, the Philippines and the Soviet Union. It involves the effort to develop structures to assure human rights. It also involves actions in regard to the rights of particular individuals and groups—the Wilmington Ten in the United States, native peoples in Canada and the United States and aboriginal peoples in Australia. It means taking seriously the rights of persons representing minority points of view in church life.

The Declaration of Human Rights

The Universal Declaration of Human Rights adopted twenty-five years ago today (December 10, 1948), was and remains a document of the highest importance. It proclaims fundamental, inalienable rights of the human family that are uncontested and urgently demand to be respected. Its very existence is a constant challenge to become fully engaged in the struggle for the creation of a truly human world. The Declaration was adopted by a United Nations much less representative of the diversity of hu-

70

man culture and tradition than is that body today. Its authors did not foresee some of the new ways in which power, wealth and technology are misused to violate the rights not only of individuals but of whole peoples. It is indeed a product of its time. It has therefore become necessary over the years to amplify and add to its provisions in other international instruments. Yet this basic "common standard of achievement for all peoples and all nations" has stood the test of a quarter century.

The fact that millions live today in subhuman conditions is not due to shortcomings in the Universal Declaration of Human Rights. It is because nations have thirsted more for power than for justice; because some. . . . have sought to increase their own share of the world's wealth rather than to promote equality among all members of the human family; and not least because Christians and their churches have more often lived with the injustice of the status quo rather than to exercise their right and duty to dissent from injustice wherever it occurs.

Those who follow Christ, who became poor for our sakes, cannot be insensitive to those who are in prison, are tortured, hunger or thirst. Our Lord said that to ignore them is to forget him.[1]

Joint Statement of the World Council of Churches and the Pontifical Commission on Justice and Peace

To the Canadian Ambassador to the 37th Session of the United Nations Commission on Human Rights

The Inter-Church Committee on Human Rights in Latin America. . . is pleased to accept the invitation to have representatives meet with you. . . . The Inter-Church Committee. . . is mandated to work with and for the churches as a Christian response to the Gospel challenge to seek justice in the relationships of human kind. Through ICCHRLA, Canadian Christians act with and for sisters and brothers struggling for human emancipation and fundamental rights in one part of the world: Latin America. We are among several arms of the Canadian churches as they seek to live the Gospel in a global community.

ICCHRLA has developed strong relationships with counterpart ecumenical, denominational and secular human rights agencies elsewhere in the hemisphere. The broad ecumenical network and direct relationships with human rights and popular organizations in many countries feed a constant flow of international reports, pleas from the relatives and friends of disappeared or imprisoned persons, telegrams alerting us to the savage torture and serious acts of repression against peasants and workers who seek to overcome economic and social exploitation.

ICCHRLA has received strong and growing support from the broad Christian and humanitarian community in Canada. During 1979–1980 our network of individuals, parish groups, teachers and clergy has multiplied in numbers and energy. The response to our urgent action appeals has been extremely encouraging. We believe that this support, complementing as it does the remarkable growth in local groups of such organizations of Amnesty International Canada, dramatically illustrates the live concern of Canadians for the situations of human rights in the global family.[2]

The Ministry of Risk
The Washington Post, September 23, 1980

A bee hovered near the middle button of Father William Wipfler's black clerical suit as he stood on the Q Street sidewalk.

He looked down slowly, his body frozen. "I hate bees," he said. "I don't mind bullets. But bees I hate."

Wipfler, 49, an Episcopal priest with a pleasant smile and intense hazel eyes, was standing on the sidewalk after a Sunday morning memorial service marking the fourth anniversary of the death of former Chilean ambassador Orlando Letelier.

Wipfler, now director of the Human Rights Office of the National Council of Churches, has pursued a ministry of risk. Last night he received one of the fourth annual Letelier–Moffitt Memorial Human Rights Awards in recognition of his work.

As a priest who works in the volatile arena of foreign governments and human rights, his ministry has taken strange turns and he says he was once targeted for death in the Dominican Republic. He has crept around Latin American towns in intricate routes to avoid being followed. He has hidden film of victims of violent government repression, and met secretly with informants. Many acquaintances and friends in his line of work have disappeared or died, he said.

"How do you alleviate—even for one hour—the suffering of one person whether they're in jail or being tortured or whatever? he asked. "I try to find the causes, and if it involves U.S. policy, ⸲ try to raise hell about it. . . ."

He looks like a typical urbane Episcopal priest in a parish where the biggest problem is Modern-America-and-the-Church.

But in Wipfler's Latin American parishes, the problem was often torture by the government. And in place of the calm clerical demeanor, "I have 16 of the 20 characteristics of a type-A personality," he said, laughing. "Gesticulating, thinking of two things at once, workaholic. . ."

At home, Wipfler is an assistant priest at The Church of the Transfiguration in Freeport, N.Y., near Kennedy airport. Churchgoers are used to having a newly released Uruguayan political prisoner or a Chilean activist from the Vicarate of Solidarity drop in.

His job with the National Council of Churches has two aspects. Abroad, he talks with people who say they have been victimized by their governments. He also talks with their families. In the U.S., he "storms the halls of Congress," talking to legislators and providing information. He confers with State Department officials about changing U.S. policy toward certain governments, and asks them to take more firm stands against violators of human rights.

His family tolerates all this with great patience and support. "My wife knows if I quit, I'd just go off in a corner and get moldy," he said. However, his wife would prefer he stay away from Paraguay for the moment. Wipfler and a lawyer named David Helfeld wrote a recently published book on Paraguay that was roundly denounced there, he said. "I think if I were to go to Paraguay now, she'd have a heart attack."

In 1955, when he graduated from General Theological Seminary, he decided on missionary work—as did a lot of his classmates. "I was into standard brands," he said off-handedly, "and it was one of the things I could have done. I just felt called."

He and his new wife went off to the Dominican Republic. . . . They stayed there for 8½ years, through two churches, through the final years of Gen. Raphael Trujillo, a regime marked by murder and torture. Wipfler says young people in his parish were often carted away to be tortured.

"I went there thinking the Christian religion had a lot to offer people in suffering," he said, "only to learn that I got a lot more than they did—a sense of hope, a sense of struggle and sharing. I learned what the word 'liberation' meant from my parish in the Dominican Republic."

By 1961, he says, he had made Trujillo's death list. . . . In May of 1961, Trujillo was assassinated. His family retained power for six months before a coup overturned them. The morning after the coup, Wipfler was stopped on his way to church by an anti-Trujillo group. They handed him a piece of paper.

"Here's the list," they said, Wipfler recalled. "I said, 'What list?' They said it was the list of people who were supposed to be killed. Apparently 20 of us were going to be done in that night before the coup. . . ."

"I'm not a hero," said Wipfler. "I do this as part of work I feel has to be done. What I do is just a piece of the movement. And a lot of it is inspired by Archbishop Romero."

Roman Catholic Archbishop Oscar Romero, who was slain last March as he was saying mass, was a popular figure and human rights activist in El Salvador. Wipfler happened to be leading an ecumenical delegation in El Salvador at the time. He spoke with the archbishop the day before he died. . . .

In Guatamala, in 1973, he confronted the defense minister with information that Wipfler said connected numerous peasant deaths to the military police there. "We had signed affidavits from the families of victims," said Wipfler. "I told him all this. We were in his office. He got red-faced, fingering his pistol in his holster and said, "What right do you have to come in here?" And for a while there I thought, 'I'm going to get it.' I really think my only visa was my collar. . . ."

Shortly after Letelier was killed in 1976, Wipfler came across some information about. . . Chilean secret police agents coming into the country. He quietly forwarded the information to a congressman whose staffer unwittingly released it along with Wipfler's name. In short order, a Chilean newspaper headline declared him an enemy of the people.

The next time Wipfler went to Chile, the immigration officer took one look at his passport and the name. "He gave me a very, very knowing smile." said Wipfler. As a safety precaution, whenever he wanted to leave the place where he was staying in Santiago, his hosts routinely took him out the back door. . . .

He can be undiplomatic. At a recent briefing on El Salvador for a handful of people, Wipfler got up in the middle of remarks by Deputy Assistant Secretary of State John Bushnell. . . and walked out.

At a meeting of Latin American ambassadors with President Carter at the United Nations, Wipfler stood in a receiving line that Carter was moving down. As the president came by, Wipfler unleashed a verbal critique of the Carter administration's manner of dealing with human rights violations. Before Wipfler could get most of it out, Carter was quickly shuttled away.

"Frustrating," he said. The eyes rolled again. "I dream about being far more aggressive in my ministry. I dream about changing the style—maybe stopping to teach for a year. But I never think about leaving."[3]

Declaration of Human Rights in Korea

Human rights are the supreme right given by God. God, who made humans according to his image, acts to liberate humanity from all sorts of bondage and to establish a society in which no humans are violated in terms of their fundamental human rights.

The Church takes the firm establishment of human rights as its highest task and believes that its historical commitment lies in establishing human rights, upon which the survival of individual persons and social development are dependent. The Korean National Council of Churches holds the Consultation on Human Rights to pursue effective ways to accomplish human rights. Out of the firm belief that the mission of the Church in Korean society is the firm establishment of human rights, the consultation adopted the following statement:

"In present Korean society, human rights are being ruthlessly destroyed. Politically the people of Korea have lost their rightful sovereignty. 'Democracy' is nothing but an empty slogan. All freedoms are suppressed. In a situation in which the people are robbed of even freedom of faith, the Church should deeply repent and abandon its past attitude of timidity and unconcern, and here affirm anew that establishment of human rights must begin with the struggle to recover freedom"[4]

*National Council of Churches
in Korea
Consultation on
Human Rights, 1973*

Cantata for Human Rights

I wish for a city
built on freedom,
a world wide open
where we can love.

I want to forge swords
into field tools
and change
sabers and cannons into bells.

I want a country without fear
where heads are held high,
I want right to reign
and the people to be heard.

I want to perform this task
of being an American:
breaking down barriers
and making brothers and
sisters.[5]

Father Esteban Gumucio

14.
In Solidarity
with the Poor

Christians keep being reminded that the gospel is good news, especially for the poor. Jesus was a peasant and the Christian church took root among many of the poorest people of the Mediterranean world. The World Council of Churches is giving increasing attention to understanding the issue of poverty and the role of the poor in the calling of the church to justice and to unity. Here is a typical passage:

The scandal of poverty in a world of abundance is crying out. Development decade after development decade passes by, but the poor are still dying. They die from starvation, from deprivation, from oppression. But it is their life and labour which create the wealth of the few.

In a world of scarcity in which everyone is in want, poverty would be a common challenge to everybody. But in a world of abundance in which many people are poor in order that a few others may stay rich, poverty—or better, wealth — is an infamy. Where the rich refuse to give up their privileges and share their plenty, their situation asks for reproach.

But the cry of this scandal does not seem to be heard. The people who have the power to change do not use their authority for justice, and in many cases use it to reinforce injustice. Even God seems to pay no heed to the prayer of the poor, as Job in his despair utters bitterly (Job 24:12).

Poverty is not an accident. It is a fundamental, incisive phenomenon in our society which destroys humanity, that is, God's creation. This phenomenon can only be attacked at its roots. The root of all evil things is, according to Paul in I Timothy 6:10, the love of money. Jesus calls it Mammon, an idol. It promises wealth, but creates poverty; it suggests humanity, and its effect is separation; it speaks of liberty, but enslaves people. It is multinational, pervasive, and demands allegiance of the hearts of humankind. And Jesus simply says: "Mammon and God cannot be served together."[1]

The concern for Third World Development is powerfully expressed through the work of the World Council of Churches' Commission on the Churches' Participation in Development. Reinhild Traitler, a staff member of the commission, describes its journey:

The ecumenical concept of development has a long history. Its root is in the 1966 World Conference on Church and Society which began the debate. Development became "the new word for peace" as the encyclical of Pope Paul VI, the Development of People, stated it in 1967. Still there was an overly optimistic tone, in line with the First United Nations Development Decade. The emphasis was upon economic growth, assuming that the gap between the rich and poor within and between nations could be closed quickly.

The Fourth Assembly of the World Council of Churches in 1968 called upon the churches to give sacrificially for the purposes of development and launched the idea of an appeal for two percent of the gross national product. Some churches, particularly in the Federal Republic of Germany, responded to this appeal even before the project was launched officially in 1970.

The World Consultation in 1970 in Montreux, Switzerland, quickly went beyond discussing projects to ask about the goals to which Christians and churches should commit themselves in a development process. Samuel Parmar, an economist from India, has greatly influenced the thinking of the World Council on issues of development. He identified social justice as the main objective of development in Christian perspective. Social justice denotes the participation of all in the benefits accruing from development. Self-reliance, not only in material terms, but also in cultural identity, people's creativity, and identification of people's own resources is involved. Economic growth is important, but in the framework of social justice and self-reliance.

This concept of development has greatly influenced the reflection and practical work of the commission. In the actual experiences which followed in the period between 1970 and 1975 we also learned that development, defined this way, is impossible without people's participation. This does not mean implementing programs already defined for them by someone else. They need to participate at each level of decision-making, however time-consuming or costly this may be. Participation understood this way is a political concept, that is, helping people achieve the power to shape their own lives. The Fifth Assembly of the World Council of Churches in 1975 affirmed this insight when it said the poor and oppressed communities themselves must be the agents and beneficiaries of development.

This led the commission to reflect on the challenge of the poor in the tradition of the churches. It was the beginning of an action-reflection process on "The Church and the Poor." Clearly, the documents and books published in conjunction with this study are not "neutral" documents. They present an effort to read Scripture and to understand the tradition of the church from the point of view of poor and oppressed peoples. The result of this effort at reading history with

the eyes of the poor is a radical challenge to churches and Christians who are by and large not identified with the poor and oppressed. The Old Testament and the Gospels show how much the poor, the powerless, the marginalized and outcasts enjoy the very special favor and protection of Yahweh. In fact, the care for the poor and the outcast, for the alien and the orphans are the very test of the righteousness of the children of Israel. This special favor is confirmed by Jesus, when he announces good news to the poor (Luke 4) and when his whole life and ministry is dedicated to establish signs of the kingdom for the poor. Of course, the kingdom is announced to all —to rich and poor alike. But for the rich it includes the challenge to rethink their relationship to the poor (Mark 8).[2]

Migrant Ministry Celebrates Sixty Years

In the coming months churches throughout the United States will be celebrating the 60th anniversary of the Migrant Ministry, a cooperative Catholic and Protestant ministry to migrant and seasonal farm workers.

Begun in 1920 with a handful of day-care centers for migrant children, the Migrant Ministry had spread by 1960 to 34 states with more than 500 full-time staff and 8,000 local volunteers. Its members did everything from

teaching to providing food and toys at Christmas, from Bible classes to recreation programs and community centers.

Later the Migrant Ministry and its successor organization, the National Farm Worker Ministry, became deeply involved in supporting the union organizing efforts of Cesar Chavez's United Farm Workers...

As Migrant Ministry staff expressed their anger about unjust wages and living conditions — and pushed for legislation to protect the migrants—such relationships [with the growers and canners who owned the farm worker camps] were strained to the breaking point. Gradually growers began to close their camps to the Migrant Ministry, while rural churches — made up mainly of farmers — expressed anxiety about the "political" thrust of the Migrant Ministry.

These tensions came to a head in the late fifties and early sixties as labor unions, churches and the Migrant Ministry denounced the slave-labor aspects of the bracero program, through which hundreds of thousands of Mexican nationals were imported for temporary work in agriculture.

In California, Migrant Ministry directors Dean Collins, Douglas Still and Chris Hartmire took what proved to be a decisive step, leading the churches into closer relationship with emerging farm-worker organizations, including Cesar Chavez's Community Service Organization.

In 1962, Chavez, his wife Helen and their eight children moved to Delano, California, to begin organizing farm workers into a union of their own. When the Delano grape workers went on strike for higher wages and a contract, Chavez asked the Migrant Ministry for help, and the battle was on.... By December of 1965 a delegation of national church leaders had visited Delano and called on employers to negotiate with striking workers. In July of 1968 the Northern California Council of Churches became the first major church group to endorse the United Farm Workers' grape boycott. In September 1968 the National Council of Churches followed suit.

"How did 'nice' church folks like us get into this complex, unrelenting, bruising, social struggle in the fields?" the California Migrant Ministry Newsletter asked.

"It started in an innocent enough way. We were trying to care about the migrant farm workers in our midst; their misery haunted us and we tried in our own way to love them.

"We tried day care centers, recreation programs, Bible classes, legislation, toilet kits, food baskets, community centers, toys at Christmas....

"It wasn't enough. The misery stayed. There even seemed to be more. The growers and the workers patronized us (some even liked us), but nothing changed.

Slowly we learned that even our best programs left farm workers dependent upon our accidental presence and passing good will. More slowly we recognized our own complicity and our special responsibility.

"We yearned for the day when farm workers would have enough strength in their own hands to fight their own battles, negotiate with their employers, control their school boards, and buy toys for their own children. That yearning led us into Delano in 1965 and into a rugged, up-and-down unionizing battle that seems to have no end.''

The Migrant Ministry's involvement in the Delano grape strike shattered almost all working relationships with local churches. Some individual pastors and lay persons interpreted the call of the gospel to be with the poor in their struggle for justice, but the primary response from growers and local churches was shock and outraged opposition.

Every denomination in California suffered a raging internal battle over the Migrant Ministry's efforts in Delano. Local Migrant Ministry committees in California slowly disappeared. More and more, California Migrant Ministry looked to the urban areas and the national churches for support.

In 1971–1972 CMM joined with several national organizations—Church Women United, the Migrant Ministry section of the National Council of Churches, Protestant home mission agencies and Catholic religious orders — to form the National Farm Worker Ministry as a related movement of the NCC.

Today the churches are involved in a two-year-old lettuce strike and boycott in California. The NFWM has coordinated a food drive for the families of strikers that has raised and spent more than $490,000. The NFWM staff expects the farm workers' fight to continue in California and Arizona, and spread to Texas and Florida in the years ahead. Justice, for the poor, it appears, takes a long, long time.[3]

A Prayer for the Rich

Why a prayer for the rich?
They have money. They also have power, brains and talent.
They have everything.
They don't need help, they are self-sufficient.

Lord, make the scales fall from their eyes!
Nevertheless, we need to pray for them;
They need to see
   that You are the only truly rich one.
Only You have life, knowledge, liberty,
   and full holiness.

A checkbook cannot be carried beyond death.
In the land of eternity only one coin is worth anything:
Love made real and lived.
The one who has become rich should be warned:
Families who are united become divided
   because of the inheritance.
The hour of dividing the inheritance is never a good one;
   it is, almost always, a terrible hour.

Lord, help all those who have become rich
   even though it may have been by their own hard work.
Convince them that the best inheritance for
   their children
   is to be a living example of justice, generous,
   free of the slavery to money.
Lord, help those whose riches are added up.
They are poor rich people
   if they do not achieve that simplicity which knows
   that it has everything,
   if they do not form that family relationship
   which never forgets
   that all people are invited to participate
   in Thy divine riches...[4]

Dom Helder Cámara

15.
Presence with Refugees

B ehold
  We are clay pigeons traveling swiftly
    and aimlessly
On the electric wire of international hate
Helpless targets in the shooting gallery
  of political discord
Dulled by the clattering shells
That rip toward us from both sides.
Perhaps we are merely incidental to the gunplay,
Irrevocably set in the dizzy pace of whining
    bullets,
Forced to travel up and down an uncertain line
The hesitating border of two countries.[1]

Ohiye Mori

Biblical Faith and the Sojourner

Hebrews 11 describes it: "By faith Abraham when he was called to go out into a place which he should after receive for an inheritance, obeyed; and he went out, not knowing where he went. By faith, he sojourned in the land of promise, as in a strange country..." The journey of Sarah, Abraham and their family is described in the context of faith—"the substance of things hoped for, the evidence of things not seen" (as the writer of Hebrews defined it). These sojourners and other "faith people" are identified by Hebrews as people "of whom the world was not worthy."

The motif of the sojourner, the pilgrim, is a continuing one throughout the Bible and Christian history. God reminds people in Leviticus 25:23 that "you are strangers, and sojourners with me." The Exodus theme is a powerful one. Mary and Joseph took Jesus to another land to escape a holocaust. The church as an instrument of mission spread from land to land. At the same time, the notion of sanctuary was one of "safe conduct" and "safety" from alien forces arrayed against refugees and exiles.

Hospitality to strangers is a persistent biblical command. Hebrews again crystallizes the teaching: "Continue to love each other like brothers and sisters, and remember always to welcome strangers, for by so doing, some have entertained angels unawares." In Matthew 25 Jesus echoes this theme — "I was a stranger and you took me in."

The hospitality to the stranger, the cup of water given is not only to the one in need; it is also a form of ministry to Jesus himself.

The poignancy of life in a new land is conveyed in the exiles who wonder, "How shall we sing the Lord's song in an alien land?" We call these newcomers "aliens" and yet, in many ways, it is the new land which is alien to them.

Christians are called to ministries of mercy and justice. "What does the Lord require of you," Micah asks, "but to do justly, love mercy, and walk humbly with your God." We are to "let justice roll down like waters and righteousness like a mighty stream."

The book of Acts and the epistles celebrate the diverse peoples who find their unity in Christ through their own cultural patterns. The whole body is enriched by the uniqueness of each part. Yet, each is interdependent with the other parts. The church is the body of unity and diversity.

The Churches and the World Refugee Crisis

A worldwide refugee disaster of unprecedented proportions is fast developing, a cumulative nightmare for many millions of men, women and children forced to flee their homes. Whole populations have become refugees from war, repression or deprivation. Semipermanent concentrations of refugees continue to accumulate in several parts of the world, but they risk being forgotten as newer refugee movements claim priority.

While some people choose to leave home, refugees do so involuntarily. The choice is forced upon them by turmoil or pervasive injustice where they live. In Africa an estimated 5 million refugees and displaced people have fled apartheid and its consequences in the southern part of the continent, or wars or oppressive regimes elsewhere. Somalia, in the Horn of Africa, has one of the highest concentrations of refugees in the world—1.5 million. In Asia, there are nearly 2 million refugees from Afghanistan in Pakistan, and at least 1.5 million people have fled wars and turmoil in Indochina. In the Middle East, a just solution for the 1.7 million Palestinian refugees remains elusive, and hundreds of thousands of other refugees and displaced persons, including many Christians, are concentrated in Lebanon, Cyprus and elsewhere. In Latin America close to 150,000 persons have sought refuge from repression in other countries, especially today in Central America. North America, Western Europe, Australia and New Zealand remain the major recipients of resettled refugees, and the recent Cuban and Haitian refugee movements have made the United States a country of first asylum.

Refugees have a natural claim on the churches. The concept of refuge is well-known in biblical thought.... It is also manifested in the life of Christ, who came to announce the Gospel to the poor and oppressed and "to free the captives." Thus for many years the churches have organized large-scale efforts to help refugees, first in Europe, then in all parts of the world. Often these efforts have been exemplary, setting the pattern for much bigger service and welfare.... Needed now, more urgently than ever before, is a truly international effort to meet the refugee challenge. Here the churches, with their essential life at the grass roots of every nation and yet with strong international awareness and ties, are called to provide new leadership.[2]

The Africa Connection

A hot wind drove across the stifling desert in the horn of Africa. Halimo, her mother and brother moved south. They hoped to find a settlement where they might find some food and water. Halimo fretted over her father, who had been drafted to fight in the Ogaden region. How would they get along without him to help? Was he still safe? When would they be together as a family again?

They had heard from fellow wanderers in the last settlement that basic necessities were available in Dooryule in northwestern Somalia. Although that was many days of dangerous and dry walking from their present location, none of them questioned making the trip. It was their only chance of survival. The last three years had been rainless; the usual grazing sites for their camels and cattle dried to a fine dust long ago. Without a herd, and their father gone, the family was dependent for the first time in its life. After many more days of foraging and begging in settlements, Halimo's family was just one day's walk from the camp. The presence of others in conditions like their own confirmed it. They were almost there!

The workers at the refugee camp in Dooryule found this drought and war-induced famine typical of other emergency situations. In no way did that reduce the sense of urgency they felt to relieve the suffering of the people there. Nor did it reduce their consciousness of how tenuous the survival of this camp and its inhabitants was. They were operating on a day-to-day basis for water supplies and those hung on a slender thread of funding from overseas. They were troubled by their knowledge that U.S. government funding for famine relief had not increased this year and might not be adequate.[3]

Litany for All Who Weep for Home

By the waters of Babylon
        we sat down and wept,
        when we remembered Zion.
There on the willow tree
        we hung up our harps. . .
How could we sing the Lord's song
        in a foreign land?

It is Lent:
Time to follow footprints
        left by a Galilean
        who found nowhere to lay his head.
Time to hear his words
        about gifts and giving,
        and little ones who thirst.
It is Lent:
Time to recall Jesus' tears
        shed on a hill
        above the city's northward gate,

Time to view desolation
    and to think long
    about warm and sheltering wings.

He loved homeplaces
    being one of the homeless,
He loved people,
    being a shepherd,
And it is Lent,
    Time to follow footprints.

By the waters we weep,
By the waters we weep,
    On the poplar trees
    we hang up our harps,
How can we sing a song
    in a foreign land?
By the waters we weep,
    by the Zambezi
    by the Limpopo,
    by the Kwando
    by the muddy wells near Seruli or Dikhil
By the waters
By the waters we weep,
    by the Mekong
    by the Dangrek
    by Lake Tonle
    by the South China Sea.
By the waters, by the waters
Our children wail by the waters
    by the bay under Kyrenia
    by the single rusting tap at Karak
    by the sullen surf at Tyre.
By the waters
By all the bitter waters
    We watch our loved ones die;
    We cannot sing the songs of home
    While our hearts break.
Millions
    are without homelands
Millions
    are without work
Millions
    are hungry

We are thirsty
We are
  cold, weak, fevered, thick with edema,
  thin with malnutrition, anemic,
  flatulent from amoeba, scaled by
  diarrhea
We cannot sing the songs of home
We cry quietly by the bitter waters
We are dying.

The harps are silent,
  hang them up
Hang them up on the willow trees
  on the palms
  on the cedars
Hang them on the mahogany trees
  on the dwarf pines
  on the desert thorns
Hang the harps high,
Maybe the wind will play loudly upon them
songs of sorrow.
Strum, Wind,
Strum on the harps
Strum the lament of the homeless.
Sound the death song of the refugees
  for a people of fat barns
  warm houses
  full bellies
  and a homeland still possessed,
Sound the song of the songless
Sound the lost psalm of Zion

Until somebody, hearing, remembers
  he loved homeplaces
  being one of the homeless,
  he loved people
  being a shepherd
Until somebody, listening, recalls
  it is Lent
  and time to follow footprints
Until somebody, caring, understands that
  "By the waters of Babylon
  We sit down and weep."[4]

16.
Beyond Racism

There is neither Jew nor Greek, bond nor free . . . but all are one in Christ Jesus" is the powerful conviction of Paul in Galatians 3. This expression of the unity of humankind has been an energizing vision for Christians over nineteen centuries. It challenges and transcends the divided state of humankind.

Racism is a major threat to the church's unity and integrity. Simply stated, racism is attributing certain characteristics to others based solely upon racial background. Although the black/white relationships in the United States understandably get major play when the subject of racism is mentioned, racism is a nearly universal phenomenon. Thus, the concern to root out this cancer is on many agendas.

Racism takes particularly demonic form in countries such as South Arica in which prejudice and racial exclusion are codified into law and territoriality. Thus, opposition to the presence of multinational corporations and lines of credit from banks draws the ire of Christian bodies in the U.S., Canada, and around the world.

A Zulu proverb says, "When a thorn gets into the toe, the whole body stoops to pick it out." Whether we like to recognize it or not, we all belong to the same human body. The thorn of racial and economic oppression must be taken out by all of us, or we shall suffer from the gangrene which poisons and destroys. We all need a surplus of discerning, caring love to remove this deathly thorn from humankind's body. We need to become the Body of Christ, the parts of which are interdependent in suffering and joy.[1]

Philip Potter

Church Action to Address Racism Issues

The churches together are taking vital, concrete actions to overcome racism. For example, the Church Council of Greater Seattle has been the ecumenical vehicle through which churches have acted to foster voluntary desegregation plans for the public schools. This concern for equality of opportunity in education is expressed by churches and church groups throughout the United States and Canada.

Another example is the role of the Church Council of Greater Seattle in active support of the fishing rights of Native Americans in Puget Sound. The action has been to secure support of long-standing treaty rights. The challenge has been successfully pursued in litigation, with the council serving as a friend in court of the Native Americans' rights. The *amicus curiae* brief of the churches was quoted in the Supreme Court opinion.

An Early Ecumenical Agenda

A special problem of critical urgency today is that of the relations between peoples of different races. Here all the deep human loyalties and prejudices which are present in both lofty and demonic form in all phases of the common life — pride in ancestry and heritage, dislike of alien peoples and unfamiliar ways, tension between more advanced and less advanced cultures, fear of contamination and desire for opportunity, economic greed and economic need — come to most extreme expression.

And there are in addition deep-seated antipathies and apprehensions peculiar to race relationship. The roots of the problem are deep and difficult of treatment. No simple or easy solution is possible. It is all the more imperative that Christians have a clear and firm grasp of the Christian truth concerning race, the nature of the present situation, and the Christian's responsibility for action.

For Christians, the starting point in this, as in every problem of human relations, is the affirmation that all are by birthright children of God created in the divine image; and therefore, brothers and sisters to one another.[2]

Oxford Conference on
Faith and Order, 1937

If the Church can overcome the national and social barriers which now divide it, it can help society to overcome these barriers. This is especially clear in the case of racial distinction. It is here that the Church has failed most lamentably, where it has reflected and then by its example sanctified the racial prejudice that is rampant in the world. And yet it is here that today its guidance concerning what God wills for it is especially clear. It knows that it must call society away from prejudice based upon race or colour and from the practices of discrimination and segregation as denials of justice and human dignity, but it cannot say a convincing word to society unless it takes steps to eliminate these practices from the Christian community, because they contradict all that it believes about God's love....[3]

First Assembly,
World Council of Churches
Amsterdam, 1948

The Second Assembly of the World Council of Churches declares its conviction that any form of segregation based on race, colour or ethnic origin is contrary to the gospel, and is incompatible with the Christian doctrine of humanity and with the nature of the Church of Christ. The Assembly urges the churches within its membership to renounce all forms of segregation or discrimination and to work for their abolition within their own life and within society.[4]

Second Assembly,
World Council of Churches
Evanston, 1954

Racism is a blatant denial of the Christian faith. It denies the effectiveness of the reconciling work of Jesus Christ, through whose love all human diversities lose their divisive significance. It denies our common humanity in creation and our belief that all ... are made in God's image. It falsely asserts that we find our significance in terms of racial identity rather than in Jesus Christ.... Racism is linked with economic and political exploitation. The churches must be actively concerned for the economic and political well-being of exploited groups so that their statements and actions may be relevant....[5]

Fourth Assembly,
World Council of Churches
Uppsala, 1968

My experience as a Japanese American growing up in Delano, California, has shaped my vision of the Kingdom. My experience is far less than that of my Black and Indian brothers and sisters. But, let me share, from who I am, that vision of the Kingdom.

My mother and father spoke of how they were laughed at and ridiculed. They were taken advantage of and exploited because they could not understand the language and, because they were afraid, they couldn't fight back. They spoke of killings but the killers were never found. In the town where I grew up we couldn't sit in the center section of the theatre. That was for white people. The Japs and Chinks and Mexicans, and Niggers had to sit on the side. I remember a time in high school when about four of us were sitting under a tree during the lunch hour. There were many trees on campus. But these white boys came and kicked us out, yelling, "Get out of here, you Japs."

Those were terrifying days after the Japanese attack on Pearl Harbor. Do you know what it might feel like to have American soldiers with guns at bay herding you into trains and trucks, standing guard over you as you were trundled off into the dark, not knowing where they were taking you or what they were going to do to you? Do you know what it feels like to be walking down a street in Chicago and have somebody spit in your face and call you a "God-damned Jap"? Some of you have been at those places and worse and you know.

But for those who have not been there, will you feel what that does to you?

You live with fear because you never quite know if and when they might decide to come at you.

You feel angry, but you dare not show your anger because you know they will beat the hell out of you.

You feel a rage, a helpless, hopeless rage that churns in your belly and you can't do anything about it.

It's out of that place that I come. And wherever there is bigotry and injustice and violations of people I feel the same fear and rage inside. . . .

Will you feel that rage when our government will turn its eyes away from the gross violation of human rights and will support instead the dictatorship of El Salvador and the Philippines, of South Korea and South Africa? Somehow will you feel that helpless, hopeless rage that churns in the belly when one's humanity is violated?

Will you feel that in behalf of women when they speak about the language that excludes them. . . . Will you hear when they say to us that our employment and economic practices discriminate against them? And, yes, in our churches, too, that, in spite of all our rhetoric, we continue to act as though a woman does not have the capacity to share with us the incredible good news that God loves us. How long? I call upon my brothers, how long will we continue to deliberately inflict this hurt upon our sisters?

I hope we can be a people who will feel the rage of these and many more who are daily victims of those in power, that we will stand alongside them, that we will embrace them.[6]

Action in Solidarity With the Aborigines

Our deliberations on the Kingdom of God theme at the conference on World Mission and Evangelism have compelled us to accept that the Gospel of Jesus Christ is Good News to the Poor, and that this message is to be proclaimed in both Word and Action.

We have had a personal encounter with the poor of Australia in the Aboriginal people of the land. We have heard the voice of the voiceless and we are challenged by the cry of the poor of Australia to demonstrate our obedience to the demands of the Kingdom of God.

The Aboriginal Australians have brought to our attention the way in which the Aboriginal people have been robbed of their land and spiritual heritage and have experienced racial and cultural genocide, and then been denied any fair share in the fruits of the society constructed with their resources.

The issues...raised include:

1) Aboriginal Australians must be the ones who define what the issues are that need to be addressed in relation to their own people.

2) Aboriginal Australians should be assisted to print and circulate information concerning their situation, instead of relying on White interpretations.

3) Aboriginal Australians need to control their own institutions and the funds given to them.

4) The rights of Aboriginal Australians to their own land and sacred sites and their right to determine their use should be protected.

5) Aboriginal Australians have the fundamental right to accede to education at all levels, preferably in the form of crash programs which will enable them to attain national education standards; this education should insist on the cultural identity and values of the Aboriginal people.

6) Aboriginal Australians should share fully in the fruits of the Australian economy and not have the highest unemployment rate.

7) Aboriginal Australians need adequate housing.

8) Aboriginal Australians need adequate health care.

9) The Australian Federal Government has failed to use its powers, granted by overwhelming public vote...to override discriminatory State Legislation.[7]

The conference identified a number of action steps through which to address these issues of racism in that culture.

Kumba Yah (Come By Here)

A Litany

Sing: Someone's crying Lord, kumba yah.

Leader: Someone's crying Lord, somewhere
            Some represents millions, somewhere is many places
            There are tears of suffering.
            There are tears of weakness and disappointment
            There are tears of strength and resistance,
            There are tears of the rich, and tears of the poor.

            Someone's crying, Lord, redeem the times.

Sing: Someone's dying, Lord, kumba yah.

Leader: Some are dying of hunger and thirst,
            Someone is dying because somebody else is enjoying
            Too many unnecessary and superfluous things.
            Someone is dying because people go on exploiting
                one another.
            Some are dying because there are structures and systems
                which crush the poor and alienate the rich.
            Someone's dying Lord
            Because we are still not prepared to take sides,
            To make a choice, to be a witness.

            Someone's dying, Lord, redeem the times.

Sing: Someone's shouting, Lord, kumba yah.

Leader: Someone's shouting out loudly and clearly.
            Someone has made a choice.
            Someone is ready to stand up against the times.
            Someone is shouting out.
            Offering their very existence in love and anger
            To fight death surrounding us,
            To wrestle with the evils with which we crucify each other.

            Someone's shouting, Lord, redeem the times.

Sing: Someone's praying, Lord, kumba yah.

Leader: Someone's praying Lord.
We are praying in tears and anger,
In frustration and weakness,
In strength and endurance.
We are shouting and wrestling,
As Jacob wrestled with the angel,
And was touched,
And was marked
And became a blessing.
We are praying, Lord
Spur our imagination,
Sharpen our political will.

Through Jesus Christ you have let us know
    where you want us to be.
Help us to be there now.
Be with us, touch us, mark us, let us be a blessing,
Let your power be present in our weakness.

Someone's praying, Lord, redeem the times.

Sing: Someone's praying, Lord, kumba yah.[8]

17.
The Community of Women and Men

The Bible has a strong sense of the interconnectedness of life. The fate of another is interwoven with mine. My shalom, my well-being, is intimately tied to that of my neighbor and to my nation and its neighbors.

The cooperation of women and men — the community of women and men — are old themes in the modern ecumenical movement. The themes have an ancient ring in the Hebrew–Christian tradition. They relate to the creation of the world as male and female — in the image of God. They relate to the struggle for equality, for celebrations of unity, community, and difference — in the one creation.

The current form of the theme takes seriously the liberation of women from ancient forms of bondage and from the systematic exclusionary patterns of sexism.

The Word of God is living and liberating to those who hear with faith and live it out in faith. The Biblical message becomes good news to each successive generation as the power of the Holy Spirit conveys this message through the study and action of Christian communities. Because the gospel speaks in ever-new ways to changing situations, we have nothing to fear from listening to it afresh as our consciousness and experience change.

The universal message of God's love for all humankind will continue to be heard through the power of the Holy Spirit, but the fashion in which it is heard depends on our willingness to speak and act the Word in ways concretely addressed to the struggles and longings of women and men today. Today, that speaking and acting can no longer ignore the existence of women as part of the people of God.

Women are no longer willing to be invisible partners either in the work and life of church and society or in the interpretation and proclamation of the gospel. The Word must be concretely addressed to their journey toward freedom as well as to that of others.[1]

Letty Russell

The language of a community mirrors the experience of its life together. Language includes words, images, myths, and concepts. In many ways, images are more powerful than concepts... Does the changing consciousness of women challenge the patriarchal conceptions of the divinity in the Christian tradition? Do we need a new language in talking to God? Is God as Father a relevant image for children growing up without a father?

How do the language, imagery and symbols of Scripture and its interpretation in the tradition and the canons of the churches influence the treatment of women in Church and society — and the way women think about themselves? How is the Scripture being misused to perpetuate and justify discrimination against women? All churches agree on the God-given equality of men and women as expressed in Galatians 3. At what point does your church fail to express equality?

What understanding of the authority of the ministry is implied in the practice of ordaining women but not admitting them to the full status of pastors or bishops, or making full use of their gifts in teaching, preaching and the administration of the sacraments? What structural changes are needed to allow both women and men who have not been ordained to participate more fully in all aspects of church life, including its decision-making processes?[2]

Why All the Fuss About Language?

I want to share some very personal feelings. I became part of the Women's Movement because I am concerned about how difficult it is for women to get credit, about the widening pay gap between the sexes, about the dashed hopes of women who sought professional careers, and about the small number of visible women in our political, economic, and religious life. But the one thing I did not understand was the concern about language: words such as "chairman," "God the Father," "mankind." Why all the fuss? It was just picky when there were bigger, more pressing issues at hand. I'm sure many of you feel that way as you hear speakers struggle awkwardly to demasculinize their language.

Today, I'm in a different place. Let me share my journey with you. Tucked away in an issue of *Redbook* magazine, I found a short story of a 3½-year-old girl who was watching "Sesame Street." Instructions for some activity were being given by the instructor to the children, and masculine pronouns were used: "First, he does this; then he does that." The little girl turned off the television set in tears because she was not included and she wanted to participate. I was struck by how easily we adults intellectualize about the generic nature of masculine words, but not that little girl — she was experiencing being unincluded, a nonperson.

My next step: I figured that if all these masculine words were really generic, it would be no big deal to use the feminine and that would also be generic. But that didn't happen! Use woman to include man — say Mr. Elizabeth Jernigan rather than Mrs. Fred Register—say she and leave out he — and it just doesn't sound right and passions rise. And when passions rise, people are invested; it is important. That said to me that things were not just casually generic. Chairman, postman, milkman — these words meant men because men held those jobs. And physicians' textbooks read "he" because they mean he, and nurses' texts say "she" because they mean she.

I began to look further and discovered the language game played by biblical translators. In the New Testament, masculine nouns and pronouns have often been substituted for the nouns and pronouns of common gender in the original Greek. Thus, in John 1:12 and I John 3:1 (KJV), we read that Jesus gives us the power to become the sons of God, whereas the Greek clearly states "children" of God. In many instances "no man" and "any man" are used instead of "no one" or "any one." For instance in I Timothy 3:5, "If a man knows not how to rule his own house," rather than "if any one knows not..." Similarly in I Timothy 3:1, "If a man aspires to the office of bishop..." rather than "if any one aspires."

Elohim, one of the many words for God in the Old Testament, is a feminine plural form. It is the plural of *Elah*, a feminine God, not of *El*, a masculine God. However, a masculine word ending ("im") is used, so in essence God is both male and female, which is in keeping with the androgynous god of that historical period. Note that Elohim is always translated *He*. The Holy Spirit is one of those feminine persons translated "he" in the New Testament. Yet the Hebrew word for spirit is feminine and the Greek word for spirit is neuter.

One last biblical story—about Phoebe. Paul says she was a "diakonos," in Romans 16:1, a word that is nearly always translated "minister." Then he calls her "prostatis," in Romans 16:2, meaning ruler. Yet in the King James Version, minister is changed to "servant" in reference to Phoebe, the only time "diakonos" is so translated in the entire New Testament. If you read the Revised Standard Version, she is a "deaconess" even though there were no deaconesses in New Testament times, when both women and men held the office of deacon. In fact, Greek has a separate word for deaconess which isn't used in the Bible. Therefore, Romans 16:1 reads, "I commend you to our sister Phoebe, a deaconess of the church at Cenchreae, that you may...help her in whatever she may require from you, for she has been a helper of many and of myself as well. In fact, it should read, "I commend you to our sister Phoebe, a minister of the church at Cenchreae, that you may help her in whatever she may require from you, for she has been a ruler of many and of myself as well." Hardly sounds the same! Please understand that I am not a biblical scholar, but I can read what scholars have written, and it has been an enlightening experience.

Then I ran into a study reported in *Human Behavior*. Over a period of time, letters were sent to people in the counseling profession. They were asked to describe a healthy male personality; some time later, to describe a healthy female personality; later again, a healthy personality. With few exceptions, the healthy male personality and the healthy personality coincided. I found that to be personally devastating.

As a result, I have become concerned about the subtle traps language sets up for us — our dreams and expectations, our stereotypes and visual images. The Blacks have taught us that: Blacks instead of niggers, women instead of broads; from eating watermelon to women drivers, from lazy and shiftless to silly and dumb.

Language not only expresses ideas and concepts, but—I think — it may actually *shape* them. Often the process is unconscious, yet I feel the role of language is so powerful in its imprint upon the human mind that even the violated group may begin to accept the very expressions that aid in its stereotyping. Thus to change them seems picky and unimportant. I would like to affirm our struggle with language and all its awkwardness. I have come to appreciate deeply the word and concept "humanity," and I hope you will too.

Language in a society doesn't develop apart from that society's historical, economic, and political evolution. Men really have been the most remembered people in history—the economic and political movers. Yet language is the mirror reflecting society's attitudes and thinking. As a society changes...in its concepts through political action and education, its language patterns must be modified to be an accurate mirror. I hope you can appreciate my journey—and that it has been helpful to your journey.[3]

Rey O'Day

The Magnificat

My soul magnifies the Lord,
and my spirit rejoices in God my Savior, for [God]...has regarded
   the low estate of...
   [the Lord's] handmaiden.
For behold, henceforth, all generations will
   call me blessed;
for [one]...who is mighty has done great things
   for me,
and holy is [that]...name.
And [God's]...mercy is on those who fear
   [the Lord]...
from generation to generation.
[God]...has shown strength [of]...arm,
...[the proud have been scattered in the
   imagination of their hearts],
[God]...has put down the mighty from their
   thrones,
and exalted those of low degree;
[God]...has filled the hungry with good things,
   and the rich...[have been sent empty away].

Luke 1:47–53

18.
Ministry with and through the Youngest

And they were bringing children to (Jesus) ...that he might touch them; and the disciples rebuked them. But when Jesus saw it he was indignant, and said to them, 'Let the children come to me, do not hinder them; for to such belongs the Kingdom of God. Truly, I say to you, whoever does not receive the kingdom of God like a child shall not enter it.' And he took them in his arms and blessed them, laying his hands upon them.'' (Mark 10:13–16)

For a variety of reasons, the youngest Christians have had a special place in the ecumenical movement from its earliest days in this century. Baptism is a sign of Christian unity and most traditions baptize their young. The youngest are understood to be part of the Christian community through the faith of their parents as well as through their baptism.

Children as Active Partners in the Christian Community

To celebrate the two-hundredth anniversary of the founding of the Sunday School by Robert Raikes a consultation was held to explore this theme. Persons came together in France from fifty-one countries and celebrated these convictions:

We confess that too often our efforts have resulted in action *to* the children and have not allowed their sharing in their own growth in faith. A variety of studies has shown that the most meaningful experiences of life are those in which the person actively participates and gains significance at his or her own level of development. We would therefore encourage congregations to evaluate current practices of worship, learning, service and outreach, to affirm those which involve children in a dynamic way, and to discover new means to include the whole family in faith.

We acknowledge that we have much to learn from children — their spontaneity of expression, their ability to see through the complexities of a situation to its underlying truth; their ability to discern our true motives, all provide valuable insights into Christ's invitation to come to Faith as a child. We have learned that children are particularly vulnerable to the problems of society—hunger, poverty, isolation, affluence, injustice, prej-udice, oppression, manipulation and war, all profoundly affect the lives of children. In situations of deprivation and oppression, the children are victimized by circumstances they are powerless to control. We need to recognize that these children are learning significant attitudes about life and Faith in the midst of crises and world conflicts.

The persons in the Christian community belong inseparably together—young and old alike—loving, serving, teaching and learning from one another. The challenge is great, but we choose to accept that challenge in Faith and action.[1]

Children as Part of the Congregation

It may sound like stating the obvious, but generally speaking, it is strongly affirmed that children have a central place in the life of the congregation. Children are to be valued and respected, seen and heard in the gathering of congregations. Nor is their posiition to be that of receiver only, for they have the right and the capacity to contribute with integrity to the congregation, and their insights are to be valued. This contributing is something of a very different order from "allowing" a child to present an item, read a biblical passage, or to recite a poem (which has been carefully chosen by an adult and approved as suitable for the occasion). It is the responsibility of each congregation to find ways of enabling and encouraging their children to make their own contributions in their own way.

The above has always been part of the theological and doctrinal position of the church. However, among Protestants and Anglicans in particular, it has been inadequately practiced in recent years. The church is again being called to face the fact that children are part of the body of Christ, with a share in the priesthood of all believers. Coming to terms with this concept could mean a reworking of attitudes and structures in the life of most congregations.[2]

101

United Nations
Declaration of the Rights of the Child

The right to affection, love and understanding.
The right to adequate nutrition and medical care.
The right to free education.
The right to full opportunity for play and recreating.
The right to a name and nationality.
The right to special care, if handicapped.
The right to be among the first to receive relief
in times of disaster.
The right to learn to be a useful member of society
and to develop individual abilities.
The right to be brought up in a spirit of peace and
universal brotherhood.
The right to enjoy these rights regardless of race,
color, sex, religion, national or social origin.

The Church Cares

The churches' concern for children takes many forms — concern for catechesis, education in church and in society, the child in the church and in society, the virility of family life, the rights of children, and the gifts of children.

All of the great issues documented in this sampler affect children—the search for a living Bible, the concern to overcome racism, sexism, and hunger; the efforts for a peaceful world and a life-giving environment, reconciliation and openness to the refugee.

Expressive of these concerns are two dimensions of the common ministry of the Texas Conference of Churches. One concerns access to public education on the part of children of un-documented workers from Mexico and other countries. The state has ruled these children ineligible for public education on terms like those of every other child in the community. Its program *Por Los Niños* is directed toward getting the state of Texas to change the law and its practice.

The conference also has a strong program to address the issue of child abuse. The program is directed primarily toward enabling congregatons to act in this arena.

The Role of Youth

One of the brilliant chapters in the history of the modern ecumenical movement is the involvement of youth in various dimensions of the life of the churches together. Ecumenical leaders early on recognized that the movement could not be effective without the input of the young from their own experience. This conviction is reminiscent of Jeremiah's call:

"Now the word of the Lord came to me saying, 'Before I formed you in the womb I knew you, and before you were born, I consecrated you; I appointed you a prophet to the nations.[1]"

"Then I said, 'Ah, Lord God! Behold, I do not know how to speak, for I am only a youth.

"But the Lord said to me, 'Do not say, 'I am only a youth'; for to all to whom I send you you shall go, and whatever I command you, you shall speak."

(Jeremiah 1:4–7)

World Youth Projects have been an especially important way for international teams of youth to assist people and churches in community projects, facility building and ministry.

From one vantage point, the young have the earliest experience of ecumenism, meeting those of various traditions and faiths on the playground and in the classroom even if not in churches. Their world transcends the limitations of our particular heritages.

There is a need, however, to help each generation of youth to experience the church in its ecumenical fulness. This was suggested in a 1978 statement of the Youth Working Group of the World Council of Churches:

As young Christians we are grasped by a faith which both challenges and sustains us. We are called to proclaim that faith in word and deed, in worship and common action. Our faith grows out of and drives us into the commandment of love of God, of neighbour and of self. And so we are committed to linking that faith with the whole of life. We recognise that faith takes root only in community and so we seek to deepen our sense of being part of the whole of God's people in united proclamation and committed action.

Today, young people in our member churches understand the faith in a variety of ways. Few have had a chance to be caught up in a vision of the ecumenical movement. Many are searching for a clearer understanding of the link between faith and action. Many are turning their backs on the institutional church, moving instead into uncritical acceptance of materialistic culture or searching for an authentic life of faith in various parachurch and other religious movements. Their energy, idealism and insights are missing from the renewal of Church and society. Now is the time to embark upon a significant new thrust in international ecumenical youth work.[3]

Prayer

Lord, the world needs
this marvelous wealth which is youth.
Help young people!
They possess the inexhaustible wealth of the future....
Do not allow an easy life to corrupt them
Nor difficulties to quench their spirit.
Free them from the worst danger of all—
That of getting used to being
Old within themselves
And only young on the outside.[4]

Dom Helder Cámara

19.
Ministry with and through the Handicapped

One of the most exciting developments of the ecumenical movement over the last few years has been a new awareness of the gifts and rights of the disabled or handicapped brothers and sisters. This movement takes three forms. Disabled persons themselves in our midst have found each other and developed a powerful voice. They press for a larger voice in church affairs, for access to church buildings and meetings, for recognition of their gifts and ministry, for a share in the public's agenda.

Second, churches and church bodies, newly aware, have modified architecture and agendas to receive the richness of this ministry and to press for equality of access.

Third, church bodies have become advocates in the public sector for employment, access, housing, transportation, and health care issues.

Handicapped people have helped the churches to think in fresh ways about faith issues. Often the concept of wholeness has been offered as the desired goal of Christians. Clearly, many disabled persons are not physically whole (perhaps none of us ever is). Their condition— and their obvious spiritual gifts— challenge many prevailing understandings of what wholeness means. The body of Christ and the body of humankind cannot be whole if patterns of exclusion prevail. Simplistic physical definitions of wholeness are challenged by the claims and witness of the disabled.

The physically and mentally handicapped remind all of us of our limitations. None is without sin. None without the grace of God can be made whole. Each of us in our diversity has special gifts of faith, service, ministry, and insight to share.

As a disabled person, I believe

that the supreme sin is to despise my being. I believe that I find God when I find myself, and that the presence of God and God's grace is found only in the affirmation of my totality. I am, and when I am, I am filled with grace. If I lose myself, I lose the world. So, too, I believe that if you lose me you lose the world. I believe that if I lose you, then I lose the world.

I believe there is only one grace, but that grace has many forms. As a disabled person, I believe that I am one form of grace. Affirm me, and you affirm all forms of grace. Deny me, deny others, deny yourself, and you deny God and the grace that is God.

In a very real sense, I believe that grace is understanding our fulness, accepting our limitations and turning them to useful purposes in order to do the best we are capable of doing.

Grace comes with time, slowly, as we accept the rigors of life, as we deal with others, as we accept others and as we accept ourselves. When we love ourselves, then we inevitably love others.

We include ourselves when we make room for others.

I believe that grace saves through faith.

I believe faith can move mountains.

I can move my hand.

That is a greater act of faith than moving mountains.

Anyone can move a mountain.

I can move my hand. As Paul wrote, "By the grace of God I am what I am, and God's grace toward me was not in vain."

I believe and know, that the disabled bring us new forms of grace, new forms of joy and sorrow, new forms of being, new forms of perception, new forms of understanding, and new insights.

If we are to survive the present time, we certainly need the new grace, perception, understanding and insight the disabled embody and bring to us.

It is a fact that we begin our lives in helplessness, and, as we age, disability will inevitably come to each of us.

To deny the disabled is to restrict and set arbitrary limits on the human experience.

To deny the disabled is to deny ourselves.

To deny ourselves is to deny God, and the grace which is God.[1]

20.
Community with Other Religious Traditions

Christians live in a multi-form world. In many cultures the majority of persons belong to other religious traditions or to none at all. Belief in the uniqueness of the Christian message does not exclude Christians from building community and taking action for human betterment with people of other convictions. Jesus with his rigorous interpretation of the claims of faith and righteousness found community with people of other nationalities and backgrounds.

The churches together have long experience of dialogue with people of other faiths and of common action to build community solidarity and seek justice.

Some rules for dialogue are suggested out of this experience.

Each partner should aim to achieve:
understanding of common and distinctive elements in each other's faith, history, and civilization;
respect for each other's religious and cultural integrity;

common commitment to strive for social justice and for responsible development of the earth's resources;

a mutually challenging enrichment of spirituality which may also be a challenge to secular neighbours.

Each partner should aim to avoid:

unfair comparison or caricature;
any attempt to impose a syncretistic solution;
covert attempts to proselytize each other;
complacency about a static co-existence;
defensive and hostile attitudes to secular neighbours.[1]

Christians in Dialogue

We are at a time when dialogue is inevitable, urgent, and full of opportunity. It is inevitable because everywhere in the world Christians are now living in a pluralistic society. It is urgent because all are under common pressures in the search for justice, peace and a hopeful future and all are faced with the challenge to live together as human beings. It is full of opportunity because Christians can now, as never before, discover the meaning of the Lordship of Christ and the implications for the mission of the Church in a truly universal context of common living and common urgency. Whether Christian or not, we must live together and do live together.

For Christians, our understanding of Jesus Christ who has assumed humanity on behalf of all persons of all ages and all cultures, confirms and authenticates this basic human demand. Christ releases us to be free to enter into loving, respectful relation with all human beings. Dialogue is but part of that encounter with others and sets the tone for all other forms of relationships, including proclamation of the Gospel, service, and the struggle for justice.

It is the grace of God that draws us out of our isolation into genuine dialogue.

In the context of dialogue with other faiths, which demands genuine openness on both sides, the Christian is free to bear witness to the risen Christ, just as the partner of another faith is free to witness to what is most important in that existence. It thus repudiates not mission as such, but merely certain one-way patterns of mission in which those who spoke and acted in the name of Christ have failed to listen to and learn from those to whom they were sent, about the latter's approach to an apprehension of reality.

We believe in the power of the Holy Spirit to lead us into all truth. This faith enables us to enter into dialogue with full openness to the truth.[2]

Christian-Jewish Relations

Christians have a special kinship with the Jewish community both because of common Scripture and tradition and because of a long history of persecution and prejudice by Christians against Jews.

This relationship takes many forms — learning about each other's traditions and high holy days, worship exchanges, common scholarship on Old Testament texts, actions to challenge the roots of anti-Semitism, and common action for social justice.

The denominations who are partners in Joint Educational Development speak of some of these issues in their "Guidelines to Alleviate Stereotyping:"

Material which deals with the *Old Testament, Judaism,* or the *Jewish people* should be especially sensitive to the tendencies toward anti-Semitism. It should enable Christian users to understand their common faith roots with the Jewish community. It should avoid implications of universal negative characteristics. Further, it should enable Christian teachers and students to learn about Judaism and the Jewish people through the period from the close of the New Testament canon through the present.[3]

Increasingly Christians have become aware of the importance of learning abut the Holocaust as a way of developing solidarity of understanding with Jewish neighbors.

Christian concerns for peace in the Middle East take special note of the uniqueness of Israel and the importance of its survival. The question of the place of Jerusalem, a city with deep significance for people of three faiths, is an important one in seeking an enlarged understanding.

Building Unity in Diversity
A Contribution from the Christian-Muslim Dialogue

The expression "unity in diversity" is well known in South-East Asian nations, all of which are faced initially at the national level with a task of forging common goals and a common identity from the rich variety of races, languages, cultures, and religions within their common borders.

Because we belong to kindred communities of faith, there are doubtless many things which Christians and Muslims can do together to foster the unity of peoples in society. Among them we can identify the following:

Achieve and maintain peace between themselves, since not only national unity but regional stability are both advanced when the different religious communities live together in peace and harmony.

Witness together for the religious and moral perspective that respects the dignity and worth of all human beings in the face of dehumanizing forces.

Unite together to strengthen the moral conscience of national endeavour — affirming those aspects of nation-building which operate for the common good, and, in obedience to God's will, calling attention to those aspects which are harmful or oppressive.

Promote together a human appreciation of the cultural achievements of all the diverse communities which make up the society — valuing those worthy achievements as the common property of the whole nation and of humanity.

Represent together the transcendent dimension of human beings in mundane society of men and women, old and young, who, in the final analysis, belong not only to this world of tir e and matter, but also to the Eternal.[4]

21.
The Continuing Ecumenical Pilgrimage

The Gospel of John ends with the verse, "But there are also many other things which Jesus did; were every one of them to be written, I suppose that the world itself could not contain the books that would be written." (John 21:25). Similarly, the expressions of Christian unity will fill countless volumes — as each congregation, community, country, region, and ecumenical structure is represented. As these pages we have shared spring to life, we see men and women, boys and girls of faith wrestling with the hard problems, sharing work and worship, working out structures to express their unity and mission. We have seen unity as gift, mandate, and the rich flowering of faith. This book has only begun to hint at all the richness of that story in each hamlet, city, and country around the world. What we do see is God's gift expressed in a myriad of colors and forms.

Find your place in it as a continuing pilgrimage, as a woman from India did at the World Council of Churches conference on Salvation Today in 1974 at Bangkok, Thailand. She described it in terms of ecstasy:

Every year when the clock strikes noon on the fifth of January my mind and thoughts will travel back to this Happy Hall where I heard at the worship service voices from Africa, Asia, Europe and America; voices of black and white, of Catholic and Protestant, rising to the throne of grace — as one voice — "Out of the depths we cry unto thee, O Lord." I have found the basic answer of unity and reconciliation here and as this united voice spreads far and wide covering the six continents we will find the wounds of suffering humanity being healed.[1]

In a church divided, in a world society divided, the Bible summons the People of God to do everything that love permits and everything that the truth requires for the growth of unity in the Church and reconciliation among all the peoples of the earth.[2]

UNITY is gift...

UNITY is calling...

UNITY is achievement...

UNITY is pilgrimage...

UNITY is for the sake of the world...

Teach us, good Lord,
to serve thee as thou deservest;
to give and not to count the cost;
to fight and not to heed the wounds;
to toil and not to seek for rest;
to labour and not to ask for any reward,
save that of knowing that we do thy will;
through Jesus Christ our Lord.[3]

Ignatius Loyola

NOTES

1. Christian Unity is a Fact

1. John Darnton, *The New York Times Magazine,* June 14, 1981, p. 32. Used by permission.
2. David M. Paton, editor, *Breaking Barriers, Nairobi 1975,* (London: SPCK; Grand Rapids, William B. Eerdmans), 1976, p. 272f. Used by permission of the World Council of Churches.
3. Donald Anderson, *The Canadian Churchman,* January 1981. Used by permission.
4. Karl Barth, *Church Dogmatics,* (Edinburgh, T. and T. Clark), 1957, Vol. iv, 1, p. 675.
5. J. Martin Bailey, *A.D.,* August 1981. Used by permission.
6. "Unity of the Church, Next Steps!" Report of the Faith and Order Conference in Salamanca, World Council of Churches, 1973. Used by permission.
7. "The Church in Poland," Source Unknown.
8. *Let's Worship, Risk,* (Geneva: World Council of Churches) 1975, p. 31ff. Used by permission.

2. Ecumenism—What's In a Word?

1. *Giving Account of the Hope,* (Geneva: World Council of Churches, Commission on Faith and Order), 1975, p. 78. Used by permission.
2. *Let's Worship, Risk,* (Geneva: World Council of Churches), 1975, p. 43ff. Used by permission.

3. The Mandate

1. Dossier for Section II, World Council of Churches Assembly, Nairobi, Kenya, 1975, Chapter II (Geneva: World Council of Churches), p. 36. Used by permission.
2. "Foundations of Ecumenical Commitment," (New York: National Council of Churches of Christ in the U.S.A.), February 1980, p. 3. Used by permission
3. Father Irènèe Beauvien, "From Talks to Cooperation," Mimeographed Essay, (Montreal: Canadian Centre for Ecumenism), January 1977. Used by permission.
4. *Your Kingdom Come,* (Geneva: World Council of Churches), 1981, p. 193. Used by permission.

5. "Jesus' Own Gift," Dossier for Section One, World Council of Churches Assembly, Nairobi, Kenya, 1975, (Geneva: World Council of Churches), p. 27.
6. *International Review of Mission*, Volume LXIX, Number 275, July 1980, p. 251. Used by permission.
7. *Ibid.*, p. 251f.

4. We Have This Ministry

1. Report of the North American Consultation on the Future of Ministry, Canadian Council of Churches and the National Council of the Churches of Christ in the U.S.A., Toronto, February 1981, p. ii. Used by permission of the Program Committee on Leadership, Division of Education and Ministry, National Council of the Churches of Christ in the U.S.A.
2. *Ibid.*, Report of the United Presbyterian Church in the U.S.A. and the Presbyterian Church U.S. delegations, p. iii.
3. "In Quest of a Church of Christ Uniting," Chapter VII, Ministry, (Princeton: Consultation on Church Union), January 24, 1980, p. 3ff. Used by permission.
4. *Let's Worship, Risk*, (Geneva: World Council of Churches), 1975, p. 27f. Used by permission.

5. The Congregation

1. *The New Delhi Report* (New York: Association Press), 1962, p. 116.
2. "Foundations for Ecumenical Commitment," (New York: National Council of the Churches of Christ in the U.S.A.), 1980, p. 19. Used by permission.
3. *For All God's People, Ecumenical Prayer Cycle*, (Geneva: World Council of Churches), 1978, p. 81. Used by permission.

6. The Search for a Living Bible

1. "Introduction to the New Testament," *The New English Bible*, (New York: Oxford University Press), 1976, p. v f.
2. Krister Stendahl, Minutes of the Unit Committee, Division of Education and Ministry, National Council of Churches, June 12, 1980, p. 1. Used by permission.
3. National Council of the Churches of Christ in the U.S.A., Office of News and Information, News Release, November 26, 1980. Used by permission.
4. Letter from Lydia DiVito, Bronx, New York. August 11, 1981. Used by permission of the author.
5. "The Netherlands—Manifesto of a Movement," Reprinted from the September 21, 1981 issue of *Christianity and Crisis*, p. 247f. Copyright 1981 by Christianity and Crisis, Inc.
6. D. T. Niles in D. J. Fleming, editor, *The World at One in Prayer*, (New York: Harper and Row), 1942, p. Used by permission.

7. Education for Liberation and Community

1. J. Somerville and C.E. Hendry, "An Affection for Diversity," (Toronto: Canadian Council of Churches), 1973, p. 15. Used by permission.

2. "Ecumenical Education," Working Paper from Education Working Group, Geneva, World Council of Churches, July 6, 1978, p. 11. Used by permission.

3. "A Stance Toward the Future," in *Doing Church Education Together: Why and How JED Works*, p. 7. Copyright 1978 by Joint Educational Development, 351 Ponce de Leon Avenue, N.E., Atlanta, Georgia 30365 and distributed by John Knox Press. Used by permission.

4. *The Final Report of the Joint Study Commission on Education*, Geneva: World Council of Christian Education and World Council of Churches), 1968, p. 42f. Used by permission.

5. David M. Paton, Editor, *Breaking Barriers, Nairobi 1975*, (London: SPCK; Grand Rapids, William B. Eerdmans), 1976, p. 90. Used by permission of the World Council of Churches.

6. "Our Schools," National Council of Churches of Christ in the U.S.A. Pronouncement, May 1980. Used by permission.

7. *Let's Worship, Risk*, (Geneva: World Council of Churches), 1975, p. 39ff. Used by permission.

8. Through Artists' Perceptions

1. Grant Spradling, "The Windmill," *An Ecumenical Journal*, Arts Issue Supplement, Terry, Montana, January-February 1981, p. 3. Used by permission.

2. Carla de Sola, *The-Spirit Moves, A Handbook of Dance and Prayer*, (Washington, D.C.: The Liturgical Conference), 1977, p. 14.

3. The Rev. Mr. Ted Robinson, Interpretive Booklet for the Seventeenth Annual Festival of the Arts, Hillcrest Congregational Church, Whittier, California, p. 1. Used by permission.

4. Livingston Biddle, "Where There is Vision," *Journal of Current Social Issues*, Volume 15, Number 3, Fall 1978, p. 84. Used by permission.

5. John D. Rockefeller III, Plaque at Lincoln Center, New York City, Dedicated June 22, 1963.

6. Wesley A. Hotchkiss, "The Windmill," Arts Issue Supplement, Terry, Montana, January-February 1981, p. 5. Used by permission.

7. Hans-Ruedi Weber, *On A Friday Noon*—Meditations Under the Cross, (Grand Rapids, William B. Eerdmans Publishing Company), 1979, p. 86. Used by permission.

8. Montana Association of Churches, Billings, Montana, Position Paper, 1981. Used by permission.

9. Mary Jane Brewster, "Dedication." Reprinted with permission from *The Witness* magazine, Ambler, Pa., May 1981.

10. "Ralph Dessem, Editor, "Guide to Contemporary Worship." (Lima, Ohio: C.S.S. Publishing Co.). Used by permission.

9. Faith, Science and Technology

1. Alfred North Whitehead, *Science and the Modern World*, (New York: MacMillan), 1925, p. 260.

2. Charles Birch, "Creation, Technology, and Human Survival," Plenary Address, Fifth Assembly, World Council of Churches, Nairobi, Kenya, December 1975. Used by permission of the World Council of Churches.

3. Paul Abrecht, Editor, *Faith and Science in an Unjust World,* Report of the World Council of Churches Conference on Faith, Science, and the Future, (Philadelphia: Fortress Press), Volume II, 1980, p. 23. Used by permission.
4. Roger L. Shinn, *Faith and Science in an Unjust World,* (Philadelphia: Fortress Press), Volume I, 1980, p. 25. Used by permission.
5. Abrecht, *op. cit.,* p. 25.
6. Shinn, *op. cit.,* p. 66f.

10. JPSS—A Slogan or a Passion?

1. "Identifying a Food Policy Agenda for the 1980s: A Working Paper," (Washington, D.C.: Interreligious Task Force on U.S. Food Policy), 1981, p. 4. Used by permission.
2. "Share Sheet," Newsletter of the Massachusetts Conference of the United Church of Christ Task Force on Southern Africa, n.d.
3. "What is the Ethic of the Use of Scarce Resources?" Abrecht, *op. cit.,* p. 160.
4. "Making a Living," Year II, Ten Days for World Development, (Toronto: Inter-Church Committee for World Development Education), 1981, p. 64f. Used by permission.
5. "Che Jesus." The prayer appeared in an anonymous flyer on urban ministry in Cordoba, Argentina, Christmas 1970.

11. Blessed Are the Peacemakers

1. First Assembly, World Council of Churches, Amsterdam, The Netherlands, 1948.
2. *The Churches in International Affairs,* (Geneva: World Council of Churches), 1979, p. 68. Used by permission.
3. *Ibid.,* p. 68ff.
4. Seattle Area Council of Churches Newsletter, May 1981. Used by permission.
5. Prayer in the public domain attributed to St. Francis of Assissi.

12. Social Responsibility in Investments

1. The Annual Report for 1979-1980 of the Task Force on the Churches and Corporate Responsibility, an ecumenical coalition of the main Christian Churches in Canada. Used by permission.
2. "Statement of Investment Policy," p. 3. Permission for the use of this material has been granted by the General Council of Finance and Administration of The United Methodist Church.
3. David Pollock, "Making a Living," Year I, Ten Days for World Development, Inter-Church Committee for World Development Education) 1980, p. 46ff. Used by permission.
4. Reinhold Niebuhr, *Venite Adoremus II,* (Geneva: World Student Christian Federation). Used by permission.

13. In Pursuit of Human Rights

1. Joint Statement of the World Council of Churches and the Pontifical Commission on Justice and Peace on the 25th Anniversary of the United Nations Declaration of Human Rights, December 10, 1973.
2. Submission to the Canadian Ambassador to the 37th Session of the United Nations Commission on Human Rights by the Inter-Church Committee on Human Rights in Latin America, January 22, 1981. Used by permission.
3. Carla Hall, *The Washington Post*, September 23, 1980. Used by permission of *The Washington Post*.
4. The National Council of Churches in Korea, Consultation on Human Rights, Seoul, November 23-24, 1973.
5. Father Esteban Gumicio, Salidaridad, Chile, December 1978.

14. In Solidarity With the Poor

1. Julio de Santa Ana, *Towards a Church of the Poor*, (Geneva: World Council of Churches), 1979, p. 30. Used by permission.
2. Reinhild Traitler, Presentation to Education Working Group, World Council of Churches, Cyprus, April 1980. Used by permission of the author.
3. National Council of Churches of Christ in the U.S.A., Office of News and Information, News Release, September 30, 1980. Used by permission.
4. Dom Helder Cámara, *Rapida*, Magazine of the Movement for Latin American Evangelical Unity.

15. Presence With Refugees

1. Ohiye Mori. Source unknown.
2. World Council of Churches Central Committee Document, Dresden Meeting, August 1981. Used by permission.
3. Bread for the World Brochure, 1981. Used by permission.
4. James A. Gittings, "Litany for All Who Weep for Home," *A.D.* Magazine, March 1980. Used by permission.

16. Beyond Racism

1. Elizabeth Adler, *A Small Beginning, An Assessment of the First Five Years of the Programme to Combat Racims*, (Geneva: World Council of Churches), 1974, p. 39. Used by permission.
2. Oxford Conference on Faith and Order, 1937. Used by permission of the World Council of Churches.
3. First Assembly of the World Council of Churches, Amsterdam, the Netherlands, 1948.
4. Second Assembly of the World Council of Churches, Evanston, Illinois, 1954.
5. Fourth Assembly of the World Council of Churches, Uppsala, Sweden, 1968.
6. Teruo Kawata, United Church of Christ General Synod, Rochester, New York, June 1981. Used by permission of the author.

7. *International Review of Mission*, Vol. LXIX, No. 275, July 1980, p. 326f. Used by permission.
8. *Let's Worship, Risk* Series (Geneva, World Council of Churches), 1975, p. 47ff. Used by permission.

17. The Community of Women and Men

1. Letty Russell, Editor, *The Liberating Word*, (Philadelphia, The Westminster Press), 1976, p. 14f. Used by permission.
2. *Workbook for the Fifth Assembly of the World Council of Churches*, (Geneva: World Council of Churches), 1975, p. 59. Used by permission.
3. Rey O'Day. Copyright 1979. Used by permission of the author. Research on God language done by the National Organization of Women Task Force on Religion.

18. Ministry With and Through the Youngest

1. Report of the Conference of Children as Active Partners in the Christian Community, Geneva, World Council of Churches, Glion, France, September 1980. Used by permission.
2. Stan Stewart, "The Church's Ministry With Children Report," Commission on Christian Education, Australian Council of Churches, n.d. Quoted in *Education Newsletter*, World Council of Churches, Vol. VI, No. 1, 1977, p. 3. Used by permission.
3. Report of the Youth Working Group, World Council of Churches, Stony Point, New York, August 1978. Used by permission.
4. Dom Helder Cámara, *op. cit.*

19. Ministry With and Through the Handicapped

1. Ron Whyte, "New Forms of Grace," *Journal of Current Social Issues*, Vol. 15, No. 3, Fall 1978, p. 61. Used by permission.

20. Community With Other Religious Traditions

1. *Christians Meeting Muslims*, (Geneva: World Council of Churches), 1977, p. 144. Used by permission.
2. *Ibid.*, p. 21f.
3. Quoted from *Liberating Words, Images, and Actions—Guidelines to Alleviate Stereotyping*, p. 4f. Copyright 1979 by Joint Educational Development, 341 Ponce de Leon Avenue, N.E., Atlanta, Georgia 30365 and distributed by John Knox Press. Used by permission.
4. Christians Meeting Muslims, (Geneva, World Council of Churches), 1977, p. 126. Used by permission.

21. The Continuing Ecumenical Pilgrimage

1. Report of the Salvation Today Conference, Bangkok, Thailand, World Council of Churches, Commission on World Mission and Evangelism, 1974, p. 45. Used by permission.
2. "Odyssey Toward Unity," (Boston: Massachusetts Council of Churches), October 1977, p. 11.
3. *For All God's People*, (Geneva: World Council of Churches), 1978, p. 93. Used by permission.